The Civil War Memoirs of Sergeant George W. Darby
1861–1865

Rogan H. Moore

HERITAGE BOOKS
2012

HERITAGE BOOKS
AN IMPRINT OF HERITAGE BOOKS, INC.

Books, CDs, and more—Worldwide

For our listing of thousands of titles see our website
at
www.HeritageBooks.com

Published 2012 by
HERITAGE BOOKS, INC.
Publishing Division
100 Railroad Ave. #104
Westminster, Maryland 21157

Copyright © 1999 Rogan H. Moore

Other Heritage Books by the author:
The Bloodstained Field: A History of the Sugarloaf Massacre, September 11, 1780
History and Genealogy of the Moore Families of Fayette County, Pennsylvania

All rights reserved. No part of this book may be reproduced or transmitted in any form or by any means, electronic or mechanical, including photocopying, recording or by any information storage and retrieval system without written permission from the author, except for the inclusion of brief quotations in a review.

International Standard Book Numbers
Paperbound: 978-0-7884-1307-0
Clothbound: 978-0-7884-9495-6

TABLE OF CONTENTS

Editorial Note 5

Preface 11

Chapter One: The Coming Struggle 13

Chapter Two: The Colonel Excited 22

Chapter Three: Gaines' Mill and Savage Station 32

Chapter Four: Soldier Pastimes 37

Chapter Five: Warrenton 42

Chapter Six: Camp Scenes 51

Chapter Seven: Fredericksburg 58

Chapter Eight: Death of Sisler 70

Chapter Nine: Incidents of the March 72

Chapter Ten: The Capture 86

Chapter Eleven: The First Escape 98

Chapter Twelve: Imprisoned Again in Libby 121

Chapter Thirteen: Woodward 132

Chapter Fourteen: Disciples of Aesculapius 137

Chapter Fifteen: Doom of the Confederacy 148

Chapter Sixteen: Salisbury 155

Chapter Seventeen: Retrospective 158

Appendix A: The 8th Regiment, P.R.V.C.
              (37th Volunteers), 1861-1864 160

Appendix B: The 191st Pennsylvania Infantry
              1864-1865 163

Appendix C: Private C. H. Golden's Experience 165

Index 179

EDITORIAL NOTE

George W. Darby enrolled as a Private in Company G, 8th Regiment, Pennsylvania Reserve Volunteer Corps, known as the 37th Volunteers, on April 24, 1861. He served continuously throughout the Civil War experiencing first-hand some of the fiercest fighting of the conflict. He was a close friend and a compatriot of my ancestor Isaac Andrew Moore (1841-1921), of Uniontown, Fayette County, Pennsylvania. Both men rose through the infantry ranks from Private to Sergeant. Both shared a bond that only those who have been through the trials of combat together could ever hope to fully comprehend. Darby's wartime experiences, encapsulated in his thoughtful memoirs, remain a powerful resource for those wishing to understand the Civil War and its impact on the lives of common people.

Darby began his Civil War memoirs in 1861, by keeping a journal which he regularly attended to whenever able. The narrative carries the reader forward to the year 1865 and contains a retrospective in which the author attempted to bring some closure to his wartime experiences. Finally completed in 1899, these memoirs appeared briefly in print under the title, Incidents and Adventures in Rebeldom. Darby's memoirs contain a treasure trove of personal anecdotes and reminiscences. In his words are to be found both the intellectual confusion caused by sectional warfare fought on a grand scale and the diabolical paradoxes of the period which remained to vex him for the remainder of his life.

The Civil War never really ended for George W. Darby, nor did it end for most of the men who fought at his side. Darby was wounded just prior to the Second Battle of Bull Run on August 28, 1862. A shell fragment exploded into his left side and reached his groin area. The wound was dressed in the field by Doctor James King, the Brigade Surgeon, at a temporary hospital established on the Gainesville Road.

This makeshift hospital was abandoned to the Confederates after Second Bull Run. During the long retreat, Darby received no medical care, except what he was able to render himself. He recovered sufficiently from these wounds to complete his three year term of enlistment in 1864, and subsequently reenlisted as a Veteran Volunteer. Sergeant Darby was honorably discharged from active duty on June 28, 1865, after four long years of wartime service.

Darby's service as a Sergeant in Company G, 191st Pennsylvania Infantry, as a Veteran Volunteer from 1864-1865, was far from uneventful. He was captured by Confederates at Weldon Railroad in Virginia on August 19, 1864, and held as a prisoner-of-war until eventually released as a paroled prisoner on March 23, 1865. He was imprisoned at Belle Isle and Libby in Virginia. Many of his comrades were sent to the Confederate prison camp at Salisbury, North Carolina.

Darby's account of prison life includes harrowing tales of attempted escapes, the agony of recapture and the brutal punishments that inevitably followed. During the winter of 1864-1865, fully one-half of all Pennsylvanians imprisoned at Salisbury either died from malnutrition and disease, or were killed outright by sadistic prison guards. Darby accurately referred to the Salisbury prison camp as a "rebel prison hell."

Darby's early writings also indicate the tendency to view the black slaves the Union Army sought after 1862 to emancipate and any "free persons of color," as objects of derision and ridicule. It is clear that Darby and many of his fellow soldiers were more determined to preserve the shattered Union than to emancipate the slaves of the south, the latter of whom were often portrayed as comic characters. That his early views on the subject of race were not atypical of the time is now widely understood and remain one of the diabolical paradoxes of his wartime experience.

It would be possible here to neatly "shift gears" towards another facet of these fascinating memoirs, but for the fact of Darby's personal metamorphosis on the question of race. Finding himself in a Confederate prison along with African-American soldiers from the experience, his attitude became greatly conciliatory. Gone from his mind were the juvenile lampoons that haunted much of his previous thinking and that manifested themselves on the early pages of his journal.

After the war, Darby returned home to his native Uniontown, Pennsylvania, and remained there until October, 1865, when he removed to Allison, Ohio. In 1870, he moved to the part of Pittsburgh which was then known as Allegheny City, Pennsylvania. He lived there for the rest of his life.

Plagued by ill health directly attributable to his wartime wounds, Darby suffered from cystitis, enlargement of the prostate gland, obesity and rheumatism. George W. Darby's life after the Civil War was filled with physical discomfort and pain. He began to suffer from incontinence and was often unable to work. Commencing on April 23, 1866, Darby drew a pension based on his military service at the rate of $24.00 per month.

On May 4, 1871, George W. Darby and Sarah E. Hutchinson were joined together in Holy Matrimony by the Reverend John B. Clark, Pastor of the Second United Presbyterian Church, which was located in the north side of Pittsburgh.

Darby was employed as a brakeman, a fireman and an engineer from 1871 to 1877, when his declining health forced him to abandon this work. He had trouble urinating and was often unable to perform his daily tasks. The simple physical process of passing water had become for him a slow and torturous ordeal. Prior to the Civil War he had worked briefly as a tanner.

George W. Darby applied for an Invalid Pension on August 25, 1892. Several friends swore in General Affidavits that he was fully deserving of this pension. A number of physicians also added their statements to Medical Affidavits on his behalf.

Darby's case was entered into Congressional Report Number 2457 of the First Session of the 59th Congress and approved on April 23, 1906. Congress agreed to grant him a pension at the rate of $24.00 per month

Darby's case was entered into Congressional Report Number 2457 of the First Session of the 59th Congress and approved on April 23, 1906. Congress agreed to grant him a pension at the rate of $24.00 per month in lieu of that which he was already receiving. In 1908, this was increased to $25.00 per month.

George W. Darby died on August 11, 1912, at his home in Pittsburgh's north side. He was born in Uniontown, the county seat of Fayette County, Pennsylvania, on February 12, 1842. At the time of his death, he was seventy years of age. After his demise, his widow, Sarah E. Darby, applied for and received a Widow's Pension based on her deceased husband's military service. This was granted at the rate of $25.00 per month. The Chief of the Finance Division of the Bureau of Pensions (then part of the Department of the Interior), was informed by Disbursing Clerk Guy O. Taylor, that a check made out to Mrs. Darby in the amount of $85.50 and dated July 4, 1920, had been returned. Sarah Darby had died on June 30, 1920.

It is my hope that Darby's memoirs will add to the well of knowledge on the Civil War. This subject surely merits such regular replenishing. The Homeric struggle recalled in these pages beckons from across the expanse of time, challenging us to learn from the past. The reminiscences that appear in these poignant Civil War memoirs deserve to be reconsidered by a new generation of Americans who would otherwise not have the opportunity to do so. Sergeant George W. Darby (1842-1912), and the veterans of 1861-1865, deserve no less.

In addition to this editorial note, there is the addition of appendices and an index. These memoirs have been fully edited and proofread in an effort to eliminate obvious problems, while attempting to preserve the narrative, whenever possible, in its original form. Darby intentionally misspelled General McClellan's surname (it appeared throughout his journal as "McClelland"), a manifestation of his vitriol for a General he came to view with jaundiced eyes. John Bierer of Uniontown, Pennsylvania, the Brigade Wagonmaster, provided Darby with a letter concerning the Maryland Campaign of 1862, some of which is included in this work. Private C. H. Golden of the Eighth Regiment, Pennsylvania Reserve Volunteer Corps, also contributed a supporting narrative. With these exceptions, this book consists solely of Sergeant George W. Darby's Civil War reminiscences.

Rogan Hart Moore
April 25, 1999
Conyngham, Pennsylvania

Preface

As the events herein narrated are true and veracious facts, no apology or excuse is necessary for their publication. Let the work be judged according to its merits or demerits. I believe that the criticism of McClellan's conduct is fully justified by the evidence produced. Enthusiastic and unreasoning hero worshippers of whom I was one of the most radical had erected General George B. McClellan upon a high pedestal of fame, loyalty and patriotism and were enthusiastically paying devotion to the shrine they had so unthinkingly erected. And yet they were unknowingly paying homage to the most secret, wily and specious traitor that the nineteenth century has produced.

He laid siege to Yorktown when its ramparts were defended by wooden guns manned by a corporal's guard of rebels. He camped in the swamps of the Chickahominy for three months while twenty thousand of his soldiers died of disease and never made an effort to take Richmond. During all this time he was howling for more men, when he well knew he had plenty of men and that the government had no more men to spare him. The Battle of Malvern Hill afterward conclusively demonstrated that there never was a time during the entire campaign when his army could not have defeated the rebel army and taken Richmond. Lee's army being defeated, he ordered a retreat on Richmond and McClellan's victorious army was ordered by him to retreat to Harrison's Landing, and thus were the victor and vanquished fleeing from each other at the same time.

On Lee being informed of McClellan's retreat, he returned and occupied the battlefield. All of McClellan's delays were purposely made by him to avoid striking a death blow at the rebellion before the rebels were fully prepared to successfully resist it. I have no motive or desire to malign the dead, but the facts as set forth in these pages are made to correct the false praise and flattery so lavishly bestowed upon this miserably incompetent general by historians and hero-worshipers; to vindicate the bravery and devotion of the noble old Army of the

Potomac; and that coming generations may know the actual truth and execrate him as his baseness and treachery so richly merit.

This work has been compiled from the vivid recollections of the events as they occurred during the Civil War and now after the lapse of thirty-four years the memory of them seems as fresh and green as though they had occurred but yesterday. I appreciate fully this grand era of brotherhood and good fellowship now so happily arrived at between the two sections of our reunited country and therefore beg indulgence from the reader for any seemingly too vigorous language which may occur within this work. The truth impels me to say that the cruelties perpetrated upon the defenseless prisoners-of-war fully justify its use.

George W. Darby
July 4, 1899
Pittsburgh, Pennsylvania

Chapter One

THE COMING STRUGGLE

There come scenes and incidents into almost every human life, which so electrify the whole being, mental, moral and physical, that the impress of them is never effaced; and so it happened, on a beautiful spring morning in the month of April, 1861. The hurly-burly of the exciting presidential campaign of 1860, when that wonderful westerner, Abraham Lincoln, had been chosen Chief Executive, had subsided, and the calm which succeeds the storm had come, and not withstanding that there was to be heard, now and then, the rumbling of complaint from the southland, which fell upon the ear of the law-abiding, peace-loving citizens of the north, like the diapason of the dying thunders when the summer shower is overpast. But alas! There was to be a fearful awakening from the supposed security, which it was thought had been secured to the nation in the election by constitutional methods, of a president who, according to usage, should preside over the destinies of the country for the term of four years next succeeding. But the institution of slavery, of which the immortal John Wesley said, "it is the sum of all villainies," had so ingrained itself into the web and woof of southern thought and action, that the people of that section had come to regard it as inseparable from their happiness and prosperity. Indeed they professed to believe, and so declared to the world, that they proposed to build a republic, the chief cornerstone of which should be the institution of human slavery, and with that fearful heresy, which had grown with their growth, and strengthened with their strength, fastened upon them, until it had become their nemesis to lure them on to certain destruction.

They trained their guns upon historic Fort Sumter, and when, at high noon on that calm and lovely April day in 1861, the lanier of that cannon was pulled, its brazen throat brayed out the challenge of rebellion, and its reverberations were heard around the civilized world. The cause of human freedom everywhere stood breathless with amazement, and although the cheeks of patriots blanched, and trembling seized their frames, it was not the blanching of fear, nor mere tremor of cowardice. Oh no! It was rather a prescience of the fearful sacrifice which they so clearly saw must be made in blood and treasure, to vindicate before the world the inspired teaching of the Declaration of Independence that all men are inherently possessed of certain inalienable rights, among which are life, liberty and the pursuit of happiness. So we say armed rebellion had thrown down the gauge of battle and thus were we of the north not only put upon our mettle as patriots, but our position was well defined. We contended no longer for the salvation of our country, and its beneficent institutions.

    As the reverberations of Ruffin's cannon went sounding through the land, waking the country from profound peace to the realities of civil war (the first shot was fired upon Sumter by Edmund Ruffin of Virginia), the whole nation, but yesterday wrapped in the habiliments of a profound peace, now flew to arms and the dread alarms of war waked the echoes of hill and dale, and from the rock-ribbed coast of New England, to the golden horn of the Pacific, preparation for the oncoming struggle was the all-absorbing order of the day. Old men upon whom advancing age had laid the heavy tribute of decrepitude, forgot their years and rushed to arms, and the youth of the land, in the first blush of young manhood, flocked to the rendezvous, and offered themselves willing sacrifices upon their country's altar, to serve and to die if need be in order that armed rebellion should be crushed out and Old Glory made again to shake her starry folds in every breeze that springs from mountaintop or billows crest over every foot of soil, made sacred by the blood of our fathers, in freedom's cause.

    With patriotic motives burning high within me, I with many thousands of my country's sons, donned the blue of a soldier boy with a faint conception of the hardship, danger and exposure we were to endure, but with a rugged and unfaltering determination to sustain our beloved country in its struggle with the cohorts of rebellion to the bitter end. I was nineteen years old, strong and vigorous, and my comrades were all young and hearty men, and with unquenchable patriotism those who survived the first three years of service with few exceptions re-enlisted for another three year term. Part of the time we were attached to the First Corps under McDowell, but the most of our service was in the Fifth Corps of the Army of the Potomac of which the Pennsylvania Reserves composed the Third Division.

On April 22, 1861, the writer enlisted in Captain S.D. Oliphant's company which was organized at Uniontown, Pennsylvania, for three month's service. On our arrival at Pittsburgh, Pennsylvania, we found the quota for the three month's men already filled, so we at once re-enlisted for three years, or during the war. I pause here to say that the company (Oliphant's), was known as the Fayette Guards, and in proof of the kind of material of which it was composed will add a list of the names of the men who were promoted from it into the three years organization by which we were absorbed:

S. D. Oliphant promoted to Lieutenant Colonel.
T. B. Gardner promoted to Major.
S. B. Ramsey promoted to First Lieutenant.
H. H. Patterson promoted to Second Lieutenant and Adjutant.
W. Searight promoted to Captain.
H. C. Dawson promoted to Captain.
H. H. MacQuilton promoted to Second Lieutenant.
J. W. Sturgis promoted to Second Lieutenant.

We were temporarily quartered aboard the river steamer Marengo, which lay at the foot of Market Street, and were drilled in a public hall at the corner of Market and Water Streets. We were boarded at the Girard House, on Smithfield Street. This hotel was at the time kept by a gentleman by the name of Fell. We were afterwards removed to Camp Wilkins (the old fair grounds), which we occupied for some length of time in common with Colonel McLain's Erie Regiment. This Erie Regiment had been uniformed in suits of gray consisting of jacket and pants, and they soon became worn and ragged, and all appeals for clothing had been refused. One genius among them whose pants had been entirely worn away at the seat, determined to appeal to the public which he did in the following original manner. It was the custom for crowds of visitors to come to camp on Sunday and the Erie man having painted the words, "The last resort," in big black letters on a large shingle, attached a cord to it and hanging it over the seat of his pants, went parading around camp among the visitors. This novel walking advertisement of their necessities soon brought the desired clothing, and I think they were mustered as the Eighty-Third Pennsylvania Volunteers.

Here we received our assignment as Company G, Eighth Pennsylvania Reserve Volunteer Company, Colonel S. Hayes commanding. Soon after we were sent to Camp Wright which was located on the Allegheny River above Pittsburgh.

After a short sojourn here we received marching orders; accordingly we were marched to Pittsburgh, where, after passing that most trying ordeal of leave-taking of the loved ones left behind, we took the cars of Liberty Street and headed for the seat of war. This was on the 21st day of July, the day of the First Battle of Bull Run. The tidings from the bloody field were flashing northward over the magnetic wires, and the news was not of a reassuring character; excitement ran high, and any man, or woman, who that day wore a smile, was looked upon with grave suspicion, and in order to put a check upon the exuberance of expression of any sympathizer with the cause of the Confederacy, there were hempen nooses decorating all of the lamp-posts along Liberty and Penn Avenues. But we sped on, and without incident worthy of note arrived at Harrisburg, Pennsylvania, where we were hastily armed with old Harper's Ferry muskets. These muskets will be remembered by the old soldiers as the gun that the boys of '61 used to say, "The fellow who stood at the butt end was in more danger than the one who was shot at." We were supplied with a few rounds each of fixed ammunition, in order that we might be ready to fight our way through Baltimore in case we should be attacked as some of the New England troops had been a few days previously, but fortunately no opposition was offered.

We remained for a few days in the outskirts of the city of Baltimore and then moved on to the capital of the nation, and encamped at Meridian Hill, where we were formally transferred from the state to the United States service, for the term of three years or during the war, said transfer being made on the 29th day of July, 1861.

The first fatal shooting accident in the regiment occurred while in camp at Meridian Hill. Our muskets had been loaded with buck and ball in anticipation of an attack from the rebel element while passing through Baltimore, and it became necessary to extract these charges. To do this a ball screw is attached to the end of the gun, screwed into the bullet and the charge withdrawn by pulling out the ramrod. A man in Company B, neglected to remove the cap from the nipple of his gun and in pulling out his ramrod the cock of his piece caught on a small pine tree at the butt of the musket, discharging it. The charge, ramrod and all struck him in the pit of the stomach and passing obliquely through his body came out at the back of his neck. I was standing nearby and ran to his assistance, but he was dead when I reached him. Our next move brought us to a place called Tennallytown where we proceeded to construct a formidable fortification known as Fort Pennsylvania, and some ten miles distant at the great falls of the Potomac, our command was inducted into the mysteries of picket duty.

I had forgotten to mention that the arrival of our command and other troops from Baltimore, at Washington, was highly opportune, as the secessionists of both these cities had become aggressive and threatening to the safety of the capital; this danger to Washington was greatly enhanced by the recent defeat of the Union forces at Bull Run. The arrival of this well organized division had the effect of restoring confidence, and assured for the time-being, the safety of the capital. The wisdom and foresight of Governor Curtin and the legislature of the state in organizing and equipping the Pennsylvania Reserve Volunteer Corp, and holding them in readiness for an emergency, was now fully vindicated. After the danger which had menaced the city had subsided, our command crossed the Chain Bridge, and built Camp Pierpont, on the south side of the Potomac River, our winter quarters. It was while we were in camp here that the battle of Drainsville was fought and won; this occurred on the 20th of December, 1861, and was the first victory recorded for the Army of the Potomac.

The prisoners here were Alabamians and they were the first rebels I had seen in armed rebellion against the authority of the United States. While at Pierpont, M. P. Miller of my company became insane from reading yellow back novels of the Claude Duvall species. Commodore Jones, of South Sea Exploring Expedition fame, owned a mansion nearby and Miller having secured a long, rusty old-fashioned navy cutlass there, belted it around him and returning to camp at dress parade, took position in rear of Colonel Hayes and with his rusty blade imitated all the movements of the colonel. Afterwards he took to the woods and running to the Potomac plunged in. He was saved from drowning and removed to the Insane Hospital at Washington, where he died.

    Grim-visaged war, horrible in all its aspects, nevertheless finds some mitigation in the character and disposition of those who make up the rank and file of its legions. Every company in all our vast army probably had one or more individuals, who, by their pranks and idiosyncrasies made even the life of the soldier on the march and in the field tolerable, by injecting something of the ludicrous into the most serious and disheartening circumstances. Well, Company D, of the Eighth Reserves, had one of the aforesaid geniuses in the person of one Bud Gaskell. This man Gaskell numbered among his varied accomplishments a mysterious power over the reptile family, and as a matter of fact he could and did handle snakes with perfect impunity. Bud was a fine specimen of physical manhood, in short he was an active athlete, and hence his practical jokes were usually endured by his victims with more complacency than would otherwise have been the case. While our command lay at Tennallytown and Pierpont, Bud in some manner secured two snakes of fair dimensions which he carried constantly about his person; sometimes in his hat, and revolting as it may seem, I have seen him with his pets in his mouth. Colonel Hayes, of the Eighth, was a special victim of Bud's pranks, and although he frequently expiated his fun by a sojourn in the guardhouse, he was insuppressible. The colonel being a man of nervous temperament, naturally hated the sight of a snake, yet Bud would approach him, extending his paw for a shake with a genial, "How do' do, Colonel," when down would come one of Bud's snakes into the colonel's hand, then of course it would become necessary for the redoubtable Bud to adjourn for the time being. I once saw this fellow approach the colonel with a snake coiled within his mouth, its head protruding from between his lips, its tongue darting out, and in order to secure the officer's attention, he says, "Granny! Let me kiss you." On this occasion the colonel was the first to beat a retreat. There being an abundance of timber in the vicinity of our camp, we had constructed cabins of a very comfortable character, from the trunks of these trees. Each one of these cabins was embellished with a huge stick chimney, daubed within and without with mud to render them fireproof, yet it not infrequently happened that the mud dried, and crumbled off, leaving the sticks exposed to the blaze. So one day as the colonel stood talking near his quarters with Captain Connor, he discovered the chimney of his cabin to be on fire. He called to his negro man to bring a bucket of water, and extinguish the flame; the negro seized the bucket of water and climbed nimbly up the corner of the building, followed closely by the ubiquitous Gaskell, who seemed so very anxious to be of service in the emergency that his motive was not questioned. But alas! Just as the negro dashed the water into the chimney, Gaskell feigned a slip of the foot and falling against the poor man, sent him, bucket and all, crashing down the chimney into the hot ashes on the hearth below. There was a wild yell from within the cabin, and instantly there sped through the door, covered hair, face and clothing with ashes, the negro, who made good time to a creek nearby, into which he plunged, thus saving himself from serious consequences from his burning clothing. Meanwhile Gaskell, to give color of accident to the matter, suffered himself to roll off the roof to the ground, whence he gathered himself up, and with distorted face and limbs, and groanings which would almost move the heart of a stepmother, limped off to his tent as though the burden of the disaster had fallen upon him. The colonel looked on in amazement and turning suddenly to Captain Connor, he asked, "Captain, where in hell did you get that damned fool?"

Gaskell, like many another soldier, was possessed of a weakness for stimulants which sometimes got the better of him. Shortly after the episode with the negro, myself with several others, among whom was Gaskell, were detailed for camp guard duty, and as we were falling into line I observed that Gaskell was counting the files from the head of the column and he finally fell in as Number 23. This number being designated as headquarters guard, of course brought the redoubtable Gaskell's beat in front of the colonel's tent, and as battalion drill was to be held that day in a field about one mile distant from the camp, our hero no doubt thought he saw an opportunity for a speculation of which he proposed to make use. Accordingly, as soon as the troop had proceeded to the drill ground Gaskell entered the tent and confiscated the colonel's whisky bottle, and proceeded at once to convert its contents to his own use. The colonel, on his return to camp, being desirous of a little something to strengthen and stimulate the inner man, proceeded to where he had left his bottle, but he looked in vain for it. He probably mistrusted what had become of it, for, coming out of his tent, he beheld Gaskell staggering up and down his beat, holding his gun to its place on his shoulder with both hands. As is usual on such occasions, there were standing about a large lot of comrades waiting to see the fun. But the colonel, not wishing to have it generally known among the boys that he was given to the use of whisky as a beverage, restrained his wrath for a short time, but it appeared that the longer he watched Gaskell, who was evidently drunk on his whisky, the madder he became, so when he could restrain his ire no longer he shouted out, "Gaskell! You damn scoundrel and thief, you stole my catsup." Whereupon Gaskell cocked his eye upon him, with a comical leer as he said, spelling the words and pronouncing them in a drawling tone, "C-a-t-s-u-p, catsup, but it wasn't that! It was r-o-t-g-u-t, rotgut." But that sort of orthography was too much for the colonel, so he roared, "Go to your tent, sir! You wooden-headed thief, you; I will allow no such scoundrel as you are to stand guard at my tent." So Gaskell staggered off to his quarters singing, "When Johnny comes marching home again," and probably as the colonel did not care to have it buited abroad that he kept whisky in his quarters, that was the last of that matter, but poor Gaskell never had the chance of standing guard over the colonel's tent again. But woe to the peddlers who frequented the camp when Gaskell was off-duty. Many a camp peddler's heels flew up, tripped by him, while their wares were scattered broadcast, to be gathered in by the hungry boys, who were ever ready to profit by Gaskell's tricks.

At Tennallytown our camp was located on a hillside, and one day a man drove in with a covered wagon, in which he had a barrel of ice cream, which he was vending at ten cents per saucer, and Gaskell was very anxious for some of that cream, but he was short the ten cents. But here again his wits stood him in good stead. He secured his game by deftly removing a linchpin from the hinder axle, and giving the horse a cut with a brush, over went the wagon, out tumbled the barrel, and starting to roll down the hill was arrested in its mad career by the ever present Gaskell. He dived into the contents of that barrel clear up to his middle, and came up smiling with his arms folded low across his breast, and a pyramid of ice cream resting upon them, which towered high above his head, and thus he made for his quarters, eating as he ran, and shedding ice cream at every jump.

Gaskell's favorite trick was to spring astride a horse behind a mounted orderly or citizen, with his snakes up his sleeves, and reaching his hands in front of the rider's face the squirming reptiles under his very nose would so affright him that he would fall from his horse into the dusty road and Gaskell after riding a short distance would slip back over the animal's rump and hanging on to his tail would reach forward his feet and lock them around the hind legs of the horse and bring him to a stop, and then dropping lightly to the ground, scamper off to avoid any unpleasant consequences.

At the Battle of Fredericksburg our command was so nearly annihilated that it was ordered back to Alexandria, Virginia, to be recruited and reorganized. During this time we did patrol duty in that city. The government had established a contraband camp at that point in which was kept several thousand negroes; it also happened that Nixson's circus had gone into winter quarters there, and Gaskell, true to his instincts managed to steal a clown's fantastic suit which was decorated with horns, fringes and bells. One evening he dressed himself in this outfit and put in a sudden appearance in the negro camp performing acrobatic feats. The terrified negroes thinking the devil himself had dropped down among them, men, women and children fled precipitately through the street, scattering in every direction. Gaskell, for this trick, was confined for a time in the slave pen. The negroes were employed by the government to perform labor on the fortifications, and many of them were so frightened that they never returned to their work again.

Chapter Two

THE COLONEL EXCITED

I will now relate two incidents which occurred at Tennallytown and Pierpont showing the excitable nature of Colonel George S. Hayes. Post Guard Number 8 was stationed immediately in the rear of the colonel's tent. The guards had been instructed, in case it became necessary for them to leave their beats during their turn on duty to call the corporal of the guard to take their place during any temporary absence. So late in the night the guard near the colonel's tent raised the cry, "Corporal of the guard Post Number 8." The cry was repeated by the next guard and so on until it reached Number 1 which was at the headquarters of the guards. The corporal jumped out of his bunk, and hastily buckling on his sword, rushed up to the guardhouse, where he found a man soundly sleeping on the ground. Roughly shaking him he demanded if he were the corporal of the guard. "No, sir," quickly came the answer. "I am the sergeant of the guard." "Well then," says the colonel. "Where in hell is the corporal of the guard?" "He's out calling the relief sir," said the sergeant. "Come with me quick," said the colonel. "There is something seriously wrong at Post Number 8." So they hurriedly made their way to the guard and the colonel excitedly said to him, "Sentry, what is the matter with you? What are you raising all this hullabaloo about?" "Why," said the sentry. "I want a drink!" "Drink! Hell and damnation," says the colonel. "Are you going to arouse the whole Army of the Potomac whenever you want a drink? Sergeant arrest that man and place him in the guardhouse. I'll learn you to want a drink while on duty." The colonel marched off to his tent, while the sentry was marched off to the guardhouse.

Another striking and ludicrous example of the colonel's excitable nature occurred at Camp Pierpont. The colonel had the regiment out drilling on a gently sloping hillside and gave the command to fire by file from right to left. Now the colonel was mounted on a horse that would not stand fire and at the first crack of a gun he turned tail and fled, notwithstanding the strenuous exertions of the colonel to hold him, but each additional shot lent wings to his flight and he carried the colonel over the hill and out of sight. Meanwhile the firing proceeded and finally the head and shoulders of the colonel could be seen above the brow of the hill excitedly swinging his sword and yelling, "Cease firing!" "Cease firing!" This was accompanied by numerous cuss words to add emphasis to his orders. But the men were enjoying the situation and could not hear his orders, and whenever they fired a new volley the head and shoulders of the colonel would suddenly disappear again. They finally ceased their fire and allowed the raging colonel to approach, who instantly ordered the regiment to camp, threatening to buck and gag the first man that fired off his gun on the way back.

I shall not attempt a description of the many battles in which we participated, only as far as may be necessary to the explanation of the incidents properly coming within the province of a work of this nature.

On learning that the enemy had evacuated Manassas, the reserves broke camp at Pierpont on 10 March 1862, and marched for that point. This march, owing to the inclemency of the weather, was the hardest, most exhausting and fatiguing that the reserves ever experienced during their term of service and was caused by the stupid blundering of someone high in authority.

This senseless and worse than useless march was made from our camp at Pierpont during one of the most terrific storms of sleet and rain which it was ever my misfortune to encounter, and to add to the aggravation of the situation, when we had almost reached Manassas, our objective point, here came the order to countermarch on Alexandria, and on reaching that point during a heavy snowfall we were loaded upon platform cars, and sent back to Bull Run. This experience was simply awful; it was a regular Burnside stick-in-the-mud with additional horrors. The roads throughout this section of the country had been transformed into rivers of mud, axle deep, and rain and sleet continued in ceaseless downpour night and day. Men, completely exhausted, fell out of rank, and dropping down in the fence corners, died of fatigue and exhaustion. I remember one night while on our return march we halted in a piece of woodland, completely fagged out, the downpour continuing; the ground was reeking with water, so that lying down was impractical. Setting to work we felled a hickory tree and building a fire against it, I sat down before it with my cap drawn over my eyes, and immediately fell asleep. On awakening I found the leathern frontis entirely burned from my cap. On resuming the march, it being impossible to follow the roads on account of the depth of the mud, we were obliged to take to the fields and woods, and as the paths formed by the advance became impassable, those in the rear would be obliged to start a new one and thus we struggled on.

Upon reaching Alexandria we were started back to the place whence we came. Now if there was ever an intelligible reason assigned for these blundering, quixotic movements, which cost the Republic vast sums of money, and the sacrifice of many precious lives, I have never heard of it. On reaching Bull Run and finding that the railroad bridge had been destroyed, a footway was constructed across the stream and we continued our march to Manassas. At that point several of my comrades and myself were fortunate enough to secure a hut which the rebels had occupied and failed to destroy when they left. We gathered a lot of wood and soon had a fire started within, which dried out the shanty and enabled us to spend a night in comfort, secure against the raging of the elements.

The next morning upon going to the site of the railroad station I saw several old locomotives which the rebels had left for the scrap pile, all of which were badly damaged; amongst them was one named "Farquier," that being the name of the county in which Manassas is located. We moved back a short distance from the railroad and went into temporary camp. In the meantime, the elements seemed to have spent their fury and the weather had become warm and pleasant. During our stay here some of our soldier boys entered a car, which lay at the station freighted with hospital stores, and proceeded to confiscate some of said goods, but unfortunately for them among the things which they stole was some wine, and of course they proceeded to fill up on this product of the vine, but, alas, it proved to be wine of antimony, and the result was that they paid the penalty of their escapade with their lives.

After a brief stay at Manassas, we marched away for Catlet Station, taking the railroad bed; and as the weather was now very hot, walking on the crossties was exceedingly tiresome and the men suffered almost as greatly from the heat on this march as they had from cold on the march of a few days previous. It was somewhat amusing to see them shed their overcoats and blankets and on coming up with an engine which a repair gang had standing near where they were repairing the track, the boys threw blankets and overcoats upon it, until it was so completely covered up that one could scarcely tell what it was. On reaching Catlet Station, we left the railroad track and taking the county road marched for Fredericksburg, but upon reaching Falmouth went into camp in a piece of pine woods in the rear of that place. The market at Falmouth was well supplied with fish of the herring variety, also with peanuts galore. This latter commodity could be purchased at five cents per peck, but as they were raw we were obliged to do the roasting act ourselves. Occasionally some of the boys who had a little remaining money would go to Falmouth and applying at a private house would secure an extra meal of herring and bacon. It had become customary among the boys in speaking of pork and crackers, to call it hardtack and sow-belly, and it had been so long thus designated that these useful articles of army diet were scarcely known by any other name. One day Sergeant Stewart, of Company G, went to Falmouth and induced a lady of the place to get him up a dinner of herring and bacon, so sitting down to the table he proceeded to dispatch his meal, which seemed to fit his appetite to a charm, when out of compliment to his hostess' skill as a cook he thoughtlessly remarked, "Madam, this is the best sow-belly I ever tackled." The lady, greatly surprised, said, "What did you say, sir?" Stewart, greatly embarrassed and blushing, said, "Oh! Ah! Excuse me. I mean to say really I think this is the best bacon I have ever tasted." While that was the best he could do under the circumstances, he did not regain his wonted composure until he was well out of that house.

The bridges had all been destroyed by the rebels, but the Yankees constructed a temporary one of canal boats until they could rebuild the railroad bridge, after which we crossed over and took possession of Fredericksburg, going into camp in the rear of the city on the heights. While we were here in camp the arsenal at Fredericksburg was accidentally blown up, supposedly by the dropping of a shell from the hand of a guard, and strange to say he was the only person killed by the explosion. There were a large number of army muskets stored in the building, which were hurled high in the air, and on coming down bayonets first, were to be seen sticking upright in the roofs of the houses. In a neglected cemetery near our camp lie the mortal remains of the mother of the first President of the United States of America, and as I stood by the neglected grave of the mother of America's great chieftain, and saw the marble shaft which had evidently been designed to perpetuate her illustrious name, lying prone upon the ground, pitted by bullet marks from rebel guns, I could but think what a sad commentary upon human greatness as exemplified in this rebel respect for the mother of the father of the country. While in camp at Falmouth we were dispatched on an expedition to the Eagle Gold Mines to block the United States ford over the Rappahannock River to prevent the crossing of rebel cavalry.

At this place Company G of the Eighth Regiment lost its first man killed by the enemy; his name was Jared Beach. He was shot and instantly killed by a rebel farmer. This cowardly murder of Beach was similar to that of the noble Elsworth at Alexandria, Virginia, but unfortunately this murder was not avenged, as the murderer made good his escape. Beach was knocking at the door when the rebel who had seen him approach the house, leveled his gun and fired through the door. The shot took effect in Beach's stomach and was fatal. This murderer's family should have been conducted to the Confederate lines, and his house and farm buildings burned to the ground. But our officers at this time strove to avoid anything that might irritate our misguided southern brethren who they hoped to coax back into the Union by soft words and gentle deeds, which as the sequel shows, was a mistaken policy, but it does seem strange how long it took our authorities to find out and realize the fact that they were dealing with desperate traitors in rebellion, who would be satisfied with no compromise, and nothing short of the complete success of their scheme of secession, and a total separation from the sisterhood of states. Virginia was at this time infested, and in fact all during the war, by a horde of natives, who were robbers and murderers by night, but who posed by day as quiet and inoffensive farmers. At night they would rendezvous at a convenient point, and under Mosby or some other guerilla leader, start out on murdering and plundering expeditions. These wanton villains ought all to have been punished with death and their property destroyed from the outset as fast as it fell into our hands.

While we were lying in the vicinity of Fredericksburg, Virginia, our camp was thronged by contrabands of both sexes, and many laughable incidents occurred, a few of which I will narrate. One day a gray-headed, venerable appearing old negro came into camp accompanied by two of his daughters, strapping wenches they were too; these he wished to hire out to the soldiers to do housework. After joking with the old chap for awhile, some soldier procured a cracker box and mounting the old negro upon it, soon had him preaching for dear life to a very mixed congregation; but his devotion was to be severely tried for when with closed eyes he knelt in prayer, someone would throw a penny on the box and instantly his eyes would fly open and he would make a frantic grab for the coin, before some other darky laid hold upon it. The next minute the soldiers would have the old preacher patting the juba and singing while the others danced. They would swing the wenches in a bewildering manner, kicking up the dust, in singular contrast with the late devotional exercises. They accompanied their dance with hand clapping and a monotonous song as follows:

>"De gals an' de boys went a huckleberry huntin'
>Fo' sho', fo' sho',
>An' out dar in de woods da seed suffin',
>Jes' so, jes' so.
>I'se gwine home to tell my mammy.
>Fo' sho', fo' sho',
>O Lord, mammy I seed sum' fin,
>Jes' so, jes' so.
>Doan' yo' see dem niggers all a comin,'
>Fo' sho', fo' sho',
>Dey gwine out of a possum huntin',
>Jes' so, jes' so.
>Dey kotched a possum but he don got away,
>Fo' sho', fo' sho',
>We doan' eat no possum today,
>Jes' so, jes' so."

With much more of the same kind the dancers were obliged to desist from sheer exhaustion. Among our negroes was one who was continually laughing. He would laugh at anything and everything; if you spoke to him he laughed, if you cursed him, he laughed, as if the joke were on you. On one occasion Comrade Jerry Jones picked up an empty gun and pointing it at him said, "Now laugh, you black rascal, and laugh hearty, or I will blow your brains out!" The negro, though badly frightened and dodging from side to side to keep out of range of the threatening gun, let peals of laughter ring out, until they woke the echoes and one would have thought his very soul convulsed with the merriest of emotions. But alas for poor Jerry! He was wounded badly in the hip at the Battle of Gaines' Mill, and in consequence honorably discharged from the service. After remaining at home and measurably recovering from the effects of his wound, he was seized with a longing to be with his comrades in the field. Accordingly he reenlisted and joined his old company and served through that most arduous campaign from Culpepper to Petersburg. While so many of the best and most hardy of our soldiery succumbed to the hardships of this campaign, Jerry passed through unscathed only to be taken prisoner at Yellow Tavern and sent a prisoner to Salisbury, North Carolina, to suffer death by slow starvation in that prison hell. Peace be to your ashes, brave, genial, generous Jerry. A fellow of infinite jest, of most excellent fancy.

On leaving Fredericksburg for the Peninsula we were marched to a point on the Rappahannock, some eight miles below the city, to a landing where a vessel awaited us.

We were accompanied by a fine brass band, in which the regiment took great pride. Upon boarding the ship, the band struck up a lively air, soon the banks of the river swarmed with negroes who could not resist the inspiring strains, and a lively dance among them was the natural result. The young negroes up to the age of sixteen or seventeen, of both sexes, were gowned in a single garment of tow cloth, constructed in the form of an ordinary nightshirt and I say to you that there were more shirt skirts fluttering in the wind that day than on the clothes line of a thrifty housewife, after a two weeks' washing! It was a most ludicrous scene and the boys cheered them on to redoubted exertion until the boat sailed away.

Among the contrabands was a boy, of about fifteen years of age, whom my messmates concluded would answer our purpose as a cook. Accordingly he was selected and installed as cook and general utility man. His name was Richmond Crutchfield and he proved to be quite original and imitative. We dubbed him Coon. He said his was a "ligious nigger," but his "ligion" soon evaporated under camp influences as was witnessed by his profanity, for he soon learned to swear like a marine, and what was worse he seemed to think that cumulative profanity would be the most useful to him, so as fast as he acquired an oath he just hitched it onto one which he was already master of and then he simply swore them all off in a string.

One day, as a flock of turkey buzzards happened to be flying over our camp, I said, "Coon, did ever you shoot a buzzard?" "No sar," says he. "I nebber did, but one of dem 'fernal things spewed on me once, sho!" "Why, how did that happen?" I asked. "Well, I'll des tell you," said Coon. "One of ole masser Crutchfield's mules, he dun gone an died. An he war layin ' in de fiel' and I go dar to fotch de cows, and dar two ole buzzards was des a pickin' away at dat ole mule's haid, an' I frowed a stone at em an' da flewed up des plum ober my haid, an' one ob dem he jes fotch a squawk, an' he spewed a whole hat full spat down on my haid, dats wat he did honey." "Why didn't you shoot him?" asked one of the boys, as soon as he could get his breath for laughing at Coon's comic account of the transaction. "Shoot him," says Coon, with a string of oaths that would have stopped a pirate ship, in mid-ocean, "Shoot him! How I gwine to shoot him when I dun ain't got no gun?"

We were landed at the White House, on the Pamunkey River, and then marched to Mechanicsville and took position on the right of General McClellan's army within sight of Richmond, the capital of the Confederacy. On the 26th of June 1862, the Battle of Mechanicsville was fought, in which the Pennsylvania Reserves only were engaged on the Union side. Back of the lines on Beaver Creek, was a considerable strip of timber, and at the first volley the negro contingent took to the woods. The rebel artillery opened upon us, but their aim was high, their shots passing harmlessly over our heads; their shells exploding in the woods, scattering the negroes in every direction. Coon had been made custodian of Lieutenant MacQuilton's fiddle, and two haversacks filled with rations. Next morning Coon put in his appearance minus fiddle or haversacks and in consequence the mess had nothing for breakfast. I took it upon myself to take him to task for the loss of the aforesaid articles when the following conversation ensued: "Coon, where are the haversacks?" "I dun frode 'em away." "Why did you throw them away?" "Gor Almighty, Mr. Darby, I couldn't run fas' 'nuf an' tote dem ar habbersacks." "Well, why didn't you hide?" "I did get nudder to hide me under a house, but hadn't been dar morn' minit fo' long com one of dem shells an' it says 'Wha is yo?' 'Wha is yo' ker bang, boom, zip!' Good God, Mr. Darby, den I had to git outen dat mighty quick, an' I was runnin' as fas' as I could an' 'long com nudder of dem ar shells, an' he say 'ketch-im, 'ketch-im, swiss-boom-whiz-z-z-z-z. Lord, Massa Darby, nigger had no bizzness roun' dar. Whar de pots an' de kittles was a bustin' an' a-tarin' up de groun', fus on dis side, den on dat side. No sar, nigger can't stan' no sich thang like dat, no sir. I codn't spar de time, or I'd frode away my shoes."

While the loss of our grub was a serious one, for we were mighty hungry after a hard battle and a night of fasting, the comical way in which Coon puckered his mouth, and by sucking in and expelling the air, gave a perfect imitation of the sounds produced by the different sized shot and shells, in their passage through the air, was so laughable that we forgave him for losing the grub.

Coon was a philosopher, too, in his way, and entertained radical and peculiar views upon the subject of emancipation. He was the only negro I ever met, who was opposed to the slaves being freed; he delivered himself upon this important topic, after this manner: "Yo' see, Marser Darby, it 'ud nebber do to make de darkies free. Now ob cose, dar am some good niggers, who will wuk, an' dar am lots of lazy niggers, dat am wuffless an' won't wuk, an dem lazy niggers, dey dest goin' ter steal all dat de good niggers make! No sar, Marser Darby, hit won't do, niggers doan wuk, when da ain't got no masser." And so far as I ever learned, Coon never changed his views upon Emancipation.

As we were being sent to Alexandria, and Coon, having developed a great aptitude for learning, we offered to send him North to school.

He respectfuly declined. Soon after this, he became separated from us. I later learned that he entered government service as a teamster. That was the last I ever heard of him.

Chapter Three

GAINES' MILL AND SAVAGE STATION

As we marched away from our camp on Beaver Dam Creek, a rebel regiment formed on the opposite bank of the narrow stream and stacked arms, neither side firing a shot.

On the 27th of June the Fifth Army Corps opened the Battle of Gaines' Mill, and through some blundering mistake our colonel, George S. Hayes, was served with an order intended for Colonel Alexander Hayes, and we were detached from the division, moved to the right and relieved Duryea's Zouaves, and the Second Regulars of Syke's Division. The Zouaves were hotly engaged when we arrived and many of them had been killed and wounded. Under a heavy fire of artillery, which killed some of our men, the regiment formed its line of battle in rear of the Zouaves and charging forward beyond their lines drove the rebels into a thick pine wood. We encountered here a murderous fire which caused our line to halt. My musket became foul and I dropped to the ground on one knee and rammed away at the cartridge with both hands to get the load down. I felt something spattering over my face and left side, and on turning around I discovered that my comrade, George Proud's head had been dashed to pieces and his brain and fragments of his skull had been scattered over me. William Kendall, another comrade next to me, was also killed while I was ramming at the cartridge, which I did not succeed in getting down. In the meantime the regiment was withdrawn and had marched away without my knowledge. Our company losses in this battle were seven killed and thirteen wounded.

Immediately after the battle we crossed the Chickahominy River, on whose banks the battle was fought, and went into camp at Savage Station. I must be permitted here to digress to say a few words upon a subject which puzzled many soldiers at the time. Why our division, armed with old useless Harper's Ferry muskets, was marched past thousands of stands of new Springfield rifles with ample ammunition in them, then forced to face the very flower of the well-armed and equipped Confederate Army. We were marched by those new and efficient arms to be hurled against our country's foe, in deadly conflict, with our facilities for doing that foe real harm minimized.

Savage Station had been made a depot of supply as well as White House Landing, and large quantities of army supplies had been concentrated at this point. The railroad bridge over the Chickahominy, a few miles away, having been destroyed, a loaded train of cars standing at the station had an engine attached to it. The throttle was opened and the engine and train sped onward and plunged over the bank into the black, slimy ooze of the Chickahominy. There had been collected at White House and Savage Station about four million dollars worth of army stores, and after the abandonment of those places, these supplies fell into the hands of the rebels, as well as some three thousand sick and wounded. Although we had fought two battles and had been without rest or sleep, and almost without food for two days, McCall's Division was selected to guard the Reserve Artillery train. With our regiments distributed among the batteries of that organization, we marched off in darkness and rain over a narrow, muddy road for White Oak Swamp. As the army was converging at this point there was congestion, confusion and delay in getting the immense trains over the one bridge, and the arrival of seven miles of batteries and wagons did not tend to lessen it any. We safely crossed, however, while the gallant Sumner held the enemy at bay and parked the artillery on the high ground bordering the swamp.

Near midnight, in the rain and pitch darkness, an officer rode up to General McCall and told him he must turn back as he was on the wrong road. The general replied that he was on the right road and would continue his march forward. About an hour later the officer again appeared and informed McCall that it was General McClellan's positive order that he countermarch his division and train to another road and allow other troops to occupy the road he was on. McCall again refused to obey the order and proceeded on his way. Now a countermarch of six miles at this time on a narrow road in darkness, mud and rain was clearly useless and uncalled for, and was simply a device of the traitorous general to allow the capture of the Reserve Artillery by the enemy. And that this view of McClellan's duplicity is not an unjust one was amply confirmed the next day. On meeting McClellan at his campfire surrounded by his general officers the next day, he took McCall aside and secretly informed him that he wished to reach the James River without fighting another battle. This he claimed he could do in twenty-four hours, provided he destroyed all his trains including private baggage. As McClellan well knew that McCall and his troops had been subjected to the greatest fatigue and hardship up to this time, he no doubt expected that McCall would gladly clear the road by destroying the trains. He had mistaken his man, however, for McCall bared his head, standing in the rain, and looking McClellan steadfastly in the eye, positively and energetically declared that he would fight over every inch of ground from there to the James River before he would destroy a single wagon. To these brave words McClellan made no reply, realizing that he had approached the wrong man, and in silence the two generals returned to the campfire.

About five o'clock in the afternoon we were relieved of the charge of the artillery and marched on the Quaker road for Newmarket, and on reaching this point the column took an old abandoned road. It became impassable in the darkness and we went into camp. In the meantime Syke's and Morrell's divisions of Porter's Corps countermarched and finding a private road passed our division in the darkness and by this means reached the Quaker road and proceeded towards the James. Porter neglected to notify our command of this movement and we were thus abandoned by our corps and commander and assumed the front the following day in the battles of Newmarket, Glendale and Charles City Crossroads.

The Eighth Reserves were placed in support of a New York German Battery which occupied the corner of a wood. A few hundred yards in our front was a frame farmhouse and to the left of the house was a dense alder patch which extended across to a wood held by the rebels. The enemy finally charged our position. At the first sight of the rebel column, although as yet they were in no danger, the cowardly Dutchmen without firing a shot, or waiting to limber up, abandoned their guns, mounted their horses and caissons and fled precipitately from the field. Standing close by, I was a witness to this disgraceful flight and yet from this incident it was reported and circulated throughout the army that the Pennsylvania Reserves had been defeated, dispersed and disorganized, which was false in every particular. This was amply proven later by General McCall on his return from Richmond, where both he and General Reynolds were taken after being captured in this battle. The charging rebels were met by counter charges from the Reserves and in the hand-to-hand struggles which ensued, numbers were killed by bayonet thrusts. In the second charge of the enemy Captain Biddle, of McCall's staff, was killed and his horse ran away, but was caught and returned by me. Colonel Hayes' horse was struck and torn to pieces by a cannon shot and the heavier portions of the animal falling upon the colonel, injured him so severely that he had to retire from the service. The loss of the Reserves in this engagement was twenty-five percent of the number engaged; twelve hundred being killed and wounded and four hundred captured.

After nightfall we were withdrawn from the field and marched to Malvern and placed in support of the line of battle on the left. As the Reserves were not prominently engaged here, they merely being held in reserve to support any weakened point, our losses were small and confined entirely to the enemy's artillery fire. During the night the army retired to Harrison's Landing. As the cowardly and despicable McClellan had already abandoned the field at Charles City Crossroads before the beginning of the battle, he also abandoned Malvern without waiting to post his lines, and skulked aboard a gunboat on the James River six miles away in perfect safety, under the empty and pusillanimous plea that he wanted to direct the fire of the gunboats. This service was evidently the duty of a staff officer or an orderly and not that of a commander of a vast army about to engage in a death struggle with a powerful foe. His duty absolutely required his personal presence on the field to direct the movements of his forces and there is no excuse for the absence of the commanding general during battle except death, disability or inability to be present. Whoever heard of McClellan making a Sheridan dash for the front? His famous rides were always to the rear! He was absent at the Battle of Mechanicsville. I did not see him and never heard of this doughty general being present on the field of Gaines' Mill, Savage Station or White Oak Swamp, and he was absent at Charles City Crossroads and Malvern Hill. And yet partisans and hero-worshipers have lauded this incompetent general to the skies.

Nothing of note occurred at Harrison's Landing except the return of those who had been captured in the campaign, the fruitless expedition of the Monitor and Galena against the rebel forts at Drury's Bluff, and a vigorous shelling our camp received one night from the enemy on the opposite bank of the James. This fire destroyed some tents and wounded a few men but the gunboats soon got their range and compelled them to hastily retire. The next day a detail crossed the river and destroyed and cleared away everything for quite a distance back to prevent any repetition of their gun practice.

Edmund Ruffin, that conspicuous traitor who had journeyed to Charleston to earn a cheap notoriety by firing the first shot at Fort Sumter, lived here and all his property was totally destroyed. And thus, partially at least, was this blatant rebel repaid for firing the shot that plunged a happy country into a fratricidal war.

Chapter Four

SOLDIER PASTIMES

Owing to Gaskell's suppleness and agility, he was the most pronounced and successful trickster, practical joker and all-round bummer in the entire command. In original invention and rapid execution of comical and mischievous tricks he was without a peer and some of them verged on the malicious, while others were so decidedly unclean and revolting they will not bear repetition in print. In this latter class of tricks I will say however, I never knew Gaskell to indulge unless under the influence of liquor.

Immediately after the Battle of Antietam we were encamped in an orchard near a brick farmhouse which stood on a hill above a very large spring at which the military balloon was inflated. As the house was supplied with water from the spring by a ram I went there one day to fill our canteens. A number of officers had ordered dinner which was being served and Gaskell wanted to take a seat at the table, but was not allowed to. He then stationed himself at the head of the stairway which led up from the basement kitchen and as the girl bearing an immense steak dish filled with meat and gravy came up he tripped her, throwing her headlong, scattering meat and gravy all over the floor. Making a hasty exit, he ran to a sutler's tent and started a raid which soon cleaned out the sutler's stock. This unjustifiable act was done by Gaskell out of revenge for being denied the privilege of eating at the first table with the officers.

Along the Potomac between Washington and Alexandria there grows in the water betwixt the shore and the channel a species of sea grass with very long slippery blades. A favorite pastime of the soldiers was to go swimming and pelt each other with balls made from this grass. By reaching down the foot and twisting it around the grass enough of it could be pulled up at once to make a ball big enough for a twelve pounder and when a hundred or more men were furiously "swatting" each other with these balls there was fun galore. Owing to their slimy, wet condition they would strike a victim with a suggestive "biff" that would raise peals of laughter at the unfortunate's expense. Gaskell, who was raised on the banks of the Monongahela, was an active and expert swimmer and diver and therefore always took an exciting interest in these battles and many a contestant would take a sudden header and disappear beneath the water by Gaskell diving and elevating his heels in the air. After these contests were over he replenished his stock of snakes by diving to the bottom of the river and overturning stones until he had secured enough for his purpose of frightening the nervous and timid and the performance of his revolting tricks.

After the Peninsular Campaign we were shipped aboard the large ocean steamer New Brunswick at Harrison's Landing for Aquia Creek. On reaching Fortress Monroe a stop was made over a mile from shore and as the anchor was being dropped, Gaskell seemingly tripped and plunged headlong overboard and began making a strangling, suffocating noise in imitation of a drowning person. His comrades who were in the secret raised the cry of "man overboard." Instantly all was excitement aboard and the captain hurriedly ordered the launching of a boat in which he took position in the bow ready for the rescue. Gaskell in the meantime had hidden behind the rudder and was watching the captain's movements closely, and when he rowed around the bow of the vessel Gaskell's cries were always coming from the opposite side. The captain finally concluded to row clear around the ship and Gaskell was discovered perched up on the rudder with an idiotic grin on his countenance, chattering like a monkey. The captain was furious and cursed and damned like a proverbial tar, finally saying: "You damned idiotic fool, I've a notion to leave you there for an hour or two!" "Go to hell," replied Gaskell."I'll be aboard before you are!" Suiting the action to the word he shinned up the rudder chains like a monkey and was aboard, very wet, but also very happy because of the trick he had served the captain. Before that official could turn his boat and get aboard, Gaskell had been effectually hidden by his comrades from the wrath of the captain.

At Pierpont, where we constructed log cabins in which to pass the winter, tricks and practical joking seemed to be the order of the day among the boys when off duty. Some of the tricks resorted to there were not only mischievous and reckless, but were actually dangerous. There was the throwing of musket cartridges which were loaded with ball and buckshot down neighboring chimneys, endangering the inmates of the cabin, to say nothing of the scattered fire. I do not remember who originated this dangerous practice, but suppose it could be charged up to Gaskell, with the chances ten to one in favor of crediting it to the right party. He was the first man I saw at this trick and Colonel Hayes was his victim.

Shortly after a log guardhouse with the universal stick chimney had been built he played some trick on the colonel which aroused the ire of that officer. He promptly arrested Gaskell and conducting him to the guardhouse placed him in confinement. A sentry paced back and forth at the door, but at the back where the chimney was there was no guard placed. As soon as the colonel's back was turned I saw Gaskell's head pop out of the chimney and wag in a very ominous manner at the colonel. As it was not getting dark I got behind a tree to await developments. Soon Gaskell appeared crawling out of the chimney. Carefully climbing down to the ground he slipped off unnoticed by the sentry, and soon reappeared at the colonel's cabin with ten rounds of ammunition which he slyly threw down the colonel's chimney. He then rapidly ran to the guardhouse and re-entered it by the chimney route and took a seat in a corner and commenced to hum a ditty seemingly too innocent and peaceful to harm a fly. The colonel, who was in the act of lighting his pipe at the fire, was liberally covered with hot coals and ashes and snorting with rage he rushed to the guardhouse evidently suspicious of Gaskell, but on seeing that innocent individual looking so peaceful and contented, blurted out, "You are here are you. You damned rascal, if you were not here I would swear it was you who threw those cartridges down my chimney!" Gaskell protested against the colonel's unjust suspicions, saying, "Colonel you put me in here for nothing and how could I do it with a guard standing over me?" The colonel, after ascertaining from the sentry that Gaskell had not been absent, walked away still muttering curses. As his form melted away in the gathering darkness the head and shoulders of the innocent and persecuted Gaskell appeared above the top of the chimney and his voice in a rollicking song followed the receding colonel.

There was a Dutchman in Company B who started a barbershop to shave the bestubbled faces of his comrades and thus rake in some extra dimes. He had a sheet iron stove in his quarters, the pipe of which he passed out near the ground, and then by an elbow it was carried up about as high as a man's head. While the Dutchman was busily engaged with a customer, David Ritchie dropped some cartridges into the stovepipe which lodged at the elbow and after awhile exploded. The stove was carried from its position and struck the Dutchman, who had his back to it, about six inches below the back, and Dutchman and stove mixed up with hair and lather went flying out the door into the company street. The air was filled with German imprecations for awhile, but as a jeering crowd soon gathered and fired cutting remarks at this mishap he soon gathered up the wreckage and retired within his cabin. In my mess was one Samuel Drumm, who is now living in Bloomington, Illinois. Sam took the cartridge throwing fever bad and many cabin fires were scattered through his agency. One day when Sturgis was lying in the bunk and I was sitting beside the fire, Sam was very active in his powder throwing, and after making a successful throw he would run into the cabin, take a seat on a back log which was lying in a corner by the fire, and laugh and gloat over the mischief he had accomplished. Joe and I discussed the dangerous practice and concluded that Sam ought to be cured of his powder throwing fever before he blew out somebody's eyes.

Taking some cartridges, I emptied their contents along the side of the back log just below where Sam always took his seat and then laid a train from his powder to a point near the fireplace. We used a club for a poker and sticking this into the fire I burnt a live coal on the end of it. Presently Sam came in and took his seat immediately over the powder, laughing heartily at the way he had made some of the boys jump. Seizing the poker I gently drew it across the train of powder; there was a flash and Sam's hilarity suddenly ended in a yell that rang throughout the camp. He snatched the cap off his head and vigorously fanned the seat of his pants as he jumped and pranced over the cabin floor like a three year old colt. Now there was a rip in the seat of Sam's pants (this fact was unknown to me), and in consequence he was blistered so that it was more comfortable for him to stand than to sit, for several days. Sam blamed Sturgis for serving him this trick and was very indignant at first, but his good nature soon returned and his malady was so effectually cured that he never had a recurrence of the powder throwing fever.

Among other pastimes of the camp were card playing, boxing, jumping, throwing in a blanket and tossing the shoulder stone. At this last exercise Lieutenant Jesse B. Ramsey, of Company G, excelled the whole regiment. He was a most powerful man. I have seen him weigh out a thousand pounds of bar iron and then lift it bodily off the scale platform. Tossing in a blanket is a most ludicrous scene and always raised shouts of laughter from the onlookers, but the fun and hilarity in the practice is never enjoyed by the victim of the tossing. Company rows and occasional personal encounters at fisticuffs enlivened the tedium of camp life, and it is safe to say that among any given number of volunteers isolated in camp life there are enterprising individuals enough to create excitement sufficient to vary the tedious monotony of it.

Chapter Five

WARRENTON

After the Peninsular Campaign, we, that is the Pennsylvania Reserves, were shipped from Harrison's Landing and disembarked at Aquia Creek, and thence marched to Fredericksburg.

After resting opposite Fredericksburg a short time we marched one night for Warrenton via Rappahannock Station. Several miles above Falmouth we became entangled in a dense undergrowth of bushes. The night was very dark and the men began to murmur and swear as they stumbled along. General Meade had command and one of my comrades yelled as he picked himself up after falling over a log, "Boys, I wonder where that goggle-eyed old fool is trying to take us anyhow?" General Meade was riding beside us and heard the remark, but without saying anything he rode forward and halting the column we went into camp and waited for daylight. As Meade always wore glasses the boys had nicknamed him "goggle-eyes," or "four-eyes," and although they yelled these names at him frequently he never paid the slightest attention to them.

On arriving at Warrenton we went into camp on a beautiful lawn which lay round about a fine brick residence. The house belonged to a gentleman whose name was Forbes who was serving at the time as quartermaster of the rebel army under General Lee. His family had fled upon the approach of the Yankees, leaving everything about the premises. Upon hearing that there was a fine library among other things in the house, I concluded I would go in and draw a book or two, as the rules in regard to returning them were not overly rigid, in short it being a game of catch as catch can. But unawares I walked into a room where General George Meade was giving some of the soldiers whom he had caught in the act of destroying the furniture Hail Columbia with variations, saying, "If you had the damned rebel who owns the property here, I would not care a damn how soon you hung him, but don't wantonly destroy property!" Then much to my gratification he added, "If any of you boys want a book to read, take it and go, but don't break up the furniture." So I walked into the library where the bookcases had been overturned and their contents scattered in wild confusion over the floor, and proceeded to select my book. I made choice of a fine copy of Shakespeare, and going to the barn got a nice pole of leaf tobacco. I returned to camp and stemming my tobacco, made it into a twist, which, together with my book, I placed in my haversack.

The next morning, August 28th, 1862, we started on the march for Manassas, and when we reached Gainesville the Johnnies opened upon us with a battery of artillery and the Second Battle of Bull Run was on. The column was halted which left Company B and G of our regiment in range of the rebel fire, and as we stood in line I was scraped by a shell which exploded after passing me, and killed Sergeant W. H. Leithhead and J. M. Wells, of Company G, and one private in Company B. It also took an arm off of W. H. Doud, of Company G, and a leg off of the adjutant of the regiment, at the same time killing his horse. My clothing, even to my shirt, on my left side, was carried away by it as was also my bayonet and haversack, Shakespeare, tobacco and all. I was painfully wounded, although not dangerously, but as we were squarely between Lee's and Jackson's armies, we were obliged to get out of there, double quick time.

After having my wound dressed, I applied for admittance to a field hospital, but it was already overcrowded, and being able to walk I returned to my command and a man was ordered by my messmates to care for me. On the third day of the battle, in accordance with previous arrangements, I retired to the rear and took up my quarters in a pine wood about two miles behind our line of battle. This wood was on the left wing of our forces. In the evening as the cook was engaged in cooking a piece of meat for our suppers, I observed the rebels dash around the left flank of our line on the very ground that General Fitz-John Porter had been repeatedly ordered to occupy by Major General Pope.

Witnessing this move as I did, and taking into account that the enemy failed to make the least impression elsewhere on our lines, I am forced to the conclusion that Fitz-John Porter was solely responsible for the loss to the Union cause of the Second Battle of Bull Run.

I narrowly escaped capture upon this occasion by taking to the bush and then prudently retreated on Washington. In a few weeks I had sufficiently recovered from my wound to resume my place in the ranks then on the march in Maryland endeavoring to head off General Lee's army. One Joseph W. Sturgis, now a resident of the city of Marietta, Ohio, was my messmate at this time. In the course of our marching we struck the National Pike at Poplar Springs, and from thence we marched on Fredericksburg. Arriving here we found General Reno hotly engaged with the Confederate forces, on the field of South Mountain.

Our division at this time being under the command of General Joe Hooker, was ordered into position at the foot of the mountain and deployed into line regardless of a murderous fire from the enemy's artillery. A charge was ordered upon the rebel line. The charging column swept grandly forward carrying everything before it and the retreat of the rebels from this field was so precipitous, and the pursuit so hot that some of the retreating enemy ran over the brink of a precipice at an abandoned stone quarry on the mountainside and were killed on the rocks below.

Sturgis was shot in the hand in the charge up the mountainside. Nevertheless, he captured a prisoner, who proved to be Major of a South Carolina regiment, and a son of the Governor of the state. Joe, after receiving the glove of the rebel Major as a pledge that he and his companion would remain where they were, started in pursuit of the fleeing enemy. He had only gone a short distance, however, when the Major's companion treacherously fired upon him, but missed. The rebel then started on a wild run down the mountain and David Ritchie, who came up at this time, took a shot at him, supposedly wounding him in the arm. The rebel, however, made his escape. On Joe's return the Major denounced the act of his companion and said he had fired without his sanction or knowledge. Joe and the Major have met since the war and renewed their battlefield acquaintance.

Sturgis, although small of stature, has the heart of a giant. "Here's to you, Little Joe, faithful playfellow, generous messmate and brave comrade. May your shadow never grow less!" But for Joe, I should probably have closed my career as a soldier early. At the Battle of Gaines' Mill my gun became so foul that it was difficult to drive the cartridge home. I dropped on my knee and was ramming away to get the load down, when I heard my name shouted and upon looking around I saw Sturgis scooting for the rear, with bullets cutting the ground about him like a storm of hail. The facts were, that in the confusion of the battle, our command had been ordered to fall back, but we had not heard the order, and were banging away at the enemy. Joe discovered the situation, and sounded the note of warning to me just in time to save me. I hesitated, upon seeing the bullets fall so thick about Joe, as to whether I should try it, but it was death to remain where I was, so I took the chance and for a marvel escaped without a scratch. The regiment by this time was out of sight, so I took the direction to the York River railroad station. Arriving there I found the boys had not reached that point, so I crossed the river on the railroad bridge and made for Savage Station, where I came up with them. They had crossed the river at Deep Bottom bridge, and gone into temporary camp at the station. I was not aware of the location of the bridge over which my comrades crossed, hence my wide detour.

The enemy's dead on South Mountain were mostly killed by shots through the head, as they were behind rocks and stone fences and could not be seen until they raised up to shoot. Our loss was very small as the rebels in shooting down the mountain fired high and most of their missiles passed harmlessly overhead.

One of the saddest incidents it was my lot to observe on this field was that of a strapping Confederate soldier who had taken refuge from the storm of battle with ten or twelve others, behind a rock, all of whom had been killed but this one. He lost both eyes, and was being led off by two of my comrades to a place of safety, and what seemed remarkable was that all those that had occupied the shelter of the rock had been killed by bullets through the head.

Immediately after South Mountain we were headed for the field of Antietam. On the 17th of September, 1862, we were drawn up in line of battle in front of the historic cornfield, which proved to be the theater of the awful holocaust of that battleground. The fire at this point was so terrific that everything was swept before it, except, here and there, a panel of fence. Here I saw a very strange sight. Some Union soldier in his excitement in loading his rifle had neglected to withdraw his ramrod, and in its flight it had struck and passed through the head of a rebel soldier and pinioned him to the fence, and there he stood stark dead.

Among the Confederate troops stationed in the cornfield was the Eighth Texas. This regiment had a large silk battle flag bearing the Lone Star, and I noticed that although there was a most destructive fire from our line directed against it, it still continued to wave, but the sequel proved that the Yankee fire had become so fierce about that standard that no man could live in it, and the color bearer had driven the staff into the ground and the regiment had divided off to the right and left of it, hoping thereby to escape the missiles of death which were hurled at it. The staff was literally riddled by bullets, but the flag continued to wave. At length one of the boys of the Ninth Reserves charged alone across the open space into the cornfield, seized the lone star flag and bore it safely back in triumph to his company.

After the battle was over, I passed over this portion of the field and found that the carnage here had been appalling. The Eighth Texas had been practically wiped out. They had fought heroically, but there lay their dead in line, officers and men, as they had fallen,

"Their backs to the field,
Their faces to the foe."

Brave men they were, but a fearful price they paid for their treason to the old flag.

Just back of the cornfield everything was in evidence of the destructiveness of our fire. I observed a rebel cannon which had been struck by a shot from one of our guns which had carried away its muzzle, while wrecked caissons, dead men and horses were heaped in wild confusion over the bloodstained ground. In passing a nearby house, I noticed a dog in the yard. He was in a kneeling position as if smelling at a rat hole, but upon closer examination he was found to be stone dead, having been struck by a stray bullet. A visit to the farmyard revealed that the farm stock, horses, cattle and hogs, had all shared the fate of the dog, and it was indeed pathetic to see their wide staring eyes, as though they had died in amazement at the horrid confusion about them. I noticed one horse in particular with its head turned; with its wide eyes fixed upon its flank, where it had received the fatal wound, as if it would inquire as to the cause of its suffering.

Upon entering the barn, I saw the floors and mows were full of dead men. The Grim Reaper of Death had gathered his human sheaves and garnered them where once had been stored the golden grain. The stable of the barn was in the basement. There, too, stalls and mangers were filled to repletion with the bodies of men who but a few brief hours before were filled with life with its varied hopes and ambitions. Surely,

"It might have tamed a warrior's heart
To have viewed such mockery of his art."

Just beyond lay a road through something of a cut, and in the depression of that thoroughfare the dead lay in winrows. Oh! The carnage of that field was awful to contemplate; look where you would the ravages of the dark-winged angel confronted you. In open field and shot-torn forest lay the mangled forms of soldiers, Federal and Confederate. Mingling in that carnival of death, the foemen of an hour ago now fraternized in an eternal peace.

There was standing, near the field of battle, a small church edifice, belonging to a denomination of Christian people, known as the Dunkards. This unpretentious house of God had stood in the range of the artillery and had been struck by sixteen solid shot which had gone crashing through it, leaving it little less than a total wreck, while all about it lay shot and shell, late the screeching messengers of death, now the mute and silent proofs of "man's inhumanity to man." Here, too, was to be found a most striking illustration of the power of education and environments; the people who were want to worship in the church above referred to were doubtless as honest and as sincere as the Christian people of the North were, yet while those of the North believed human slavery to be the "sum of all villainies," and as such prayed God for its uprooting and banishment from the face of the earth, those of the Southland believed it to be a divine institution, and so proclaimed it to be, and prayed earnestly to the same Heavenly Father for its preservation, and that it might live and spread itself over all the domain of our country. But just how it could be, that men had come to believe that they had the right to ignore the Divine declaration that, "In the sweat of thy brow shalt thou eat thy bread," and to transfer to others the responsibility of doing so for them, is not so clear to us. But, sure it is, that they professed so to believe; and they hesitated not to supplement their faith by cruelly lashing the bare backs of their slaves, thus outraging every principle of human justice, until the arbitrament of the sword seemed the court of last appeal and the blackened faces of the dead on the field of Antietam, staring vacantly in the face of high heaven, protested mutely against such unchristian savagery.

After the Battle of Antietam had been fought and won, as it was by the Federals, the rebel army was truly in a most deplorable condition, having been beaten and shattered at every point. It was penned in a bend of the Potomac River, without bridge or other means of crossing, and the army of Lee was at the mercy of General George B. McClellan. But that doughty commander, who had received by common consent the nom de plume of the "Unready," was true to his instincts, and granted General Lee a suspension of hostilities for the space of twenty-four hours, ostensibly in which to bury his dead. This was really in which to lay pontoons and escape with his badly whipped and beaten army, thus bearing off the garland of victory which rightfully should have graced the Federal brow. The battle was fairly won by the boys in blue, notwithstanding, as I do truly and sincerely believe, against the desire, and intention of our commanding General, for McClellan in his attempt to justify his conduct, and to excuse himself for not gathering up the fruits of the victory, which his gallant army in spite of his own pusillanimous conduct, had gloriously won, said he was short of artillery ammunition. He also pleaded the losses which he had sustained in killed and wounded, both of which excuses were untrue and unfounded. John Bierer, who was a member of my company, and is now living at Uniontown, Pennsylvania, and whose verification of the truth of this statement can be had anyday, was on the day of the battle brigade wagonmaster, in charge of the reserve artillery train of ammunition and had his wagons on the ground just where they were needed, and with plenty of ammunition from first to last.

The following statements of facts quoted from a letter received by me from Comrade Bierer are in his own words and I will say that this statement exactly coincides with the facts as narrated by him to me at Antietam a few days after the battle: "I was brigade wagonmaster at the time. Had charge of ninety-six wagons loaded full of ammunition for musketry, rifles and cannon when we left Washington D.C., on the 8th and Rockville on the 10th of September, 1862, for the campaign in Maryland. Was at the foot of South Mountain on the morning of the 12th in time for the battle, with my entire train of wagons. Unloaded two wagons to supply Meade's Division before you went up the mountain, and sent one with small and two with heavy ammunition to supply the troops on the left of the pike. The next morning with ninety-one full and five empty or partly emptied wagons, we started about nine o'clock, moving to the left of the pike, crossed South Mountain, and on the evening of the 16th at dusk crossed Sharpsburg bridge and camped by the old mill to the left of the Williamsport pike. The next morning early I sent two wagons up the pike to Sumner, two crossed the bridge, turned to the left and went to supply Hooker and the reserves and four wagons were sent to Burnside. In all during the battles of South Mountain and Antietam, thirteen wagons of ammunition were unloaded, or partly so, leaving me eighty-three wagons of ammunition untouched."

Now when we recollect that all the divisions of the army had trains of ammunition of their own in addition to this reserve artillery train, it is easily seen from this detailed statement of Captain Bierer that there was no lack of ammunition in the Army of the Potomac at anytime during the Maryland campaign. As to McClellan's other excuses, viz., the losses his army had sustained and his desire to enable the rebels to bury their dead, I will say that the rebels met with losses also and were not being reinforced as was McClellan's army. And as for the dead, a dead rebel could lie unburied just as long as a dead Yank. I was in line in front of the cornfield when the order to cease firing was received and I well remember the dismay and consternation it produced among the rank and file. "Why do we cease firing when we have the enemy whipped?" and "We can drive the whole rebel army into the Potomac," and kindred ejaculations were heard on every side, but a continuation of the conflict meant the destruction of Lee's army and McClellan's only possible way to avoid this contingency and save the rebel cause with which he secretly sympathized was to order a sudden cessation of hostilities. I also met and talked with new soldiers the evening after the battle who had not had a chance to discharge a gun at the enemy that day, and I know, and thousands of other soldiers who participated in that fight know, that reinforcements were arriving in large numbers during that eventful day.

In common with the rank and file of the eastern army, up to this time, I had been an enthusiastic McClellan admirer, but the facts above stated, taken in connection with the stupid conduct of the Peninsular Campaign set the seal upon General George B. McClellan as the chief traitor of the nineteenth century, and if any confirmation of this opinion as to his character were necessary, it was furnished by the general solicitude exhibited on the part of the rebels at Richmond, on his behalf, which I observed while a prisoner of war there.

Chapter Six

CAMP SCENES

After the Battle of Antietam our command went into camp in an orchard near a brick house which stood on an elevation, and just below it, in the valley, gushed one of the largest flowing springs it was ever my good fortune to see. As Gaskell was pitching his tent in the orchard, in making the necessary elevation, he unearthed an arm, and grasping the hand as he might that of a living comrade, exclaimed, "Hello, old fellow, how do you do. How is it down there any-how?" He then calmly proceeded with his work.

A short distance below the spring were some buildings which the rebels were occupying as hospitals. Out in the open air was an operating table, where amputations were being performed. Arms and legs by the cartload had been dissevered, some of which had been buried. It was one of those which Gaskell disturbed while engaged in pitching his tent.

There were large numbers of sightseers and relic hunters visiting the battlefield at this time, and some gruesome sights they saw, I can assure you. As I was going to the spring for water on one occasion, the surgeon was preparing to amputate a leg, and as I halted to observe the operation, a civilian who had come to see the sights, was also standing near. The rebel surgeon, his sleeves rolled up like a butcher in the shambles, displayed his shining scalpel and with one sweeping stroke, severed the muscles to the bone, around the entire circumference of the limb. At this sight down went the civilian in a dead faint. I dashed the contents of my canteen in his face. He revived, but with an expression of horror upon his face which I shall never forget, exclaimed, "My God, this is terrible!" He hurriedly left the place.

Now gentle reader, I imagine hearing you say how much gentler and more kindly must have been the heart of this civilian than that of the man Gaskell. Not so. The one was inured to such sights, and the other was not. That was all the difference. Probably the man Gaskell would have rushed to the rescue of a suffering person just as readily and as sympathetically as the other. There seems to be an innate disposition in the human mind to adapt itself to its environment, and to make the best of its surroundings. The soldier knows from the nature of his calling that he will be called upon to see and undergo sufferings which are not common to civil life, and by a merciful provision of nature or Providence, he undergoes the transition almost imperceptibly.

But it is truly remarkable into what risks and adventures curiosity will lead the average human being. One day a young man with his family, consisting of his wife and one child, a bright little girl, drove onto the field, which was thickly strewn with the debris of battle, and wishing to carry off some memento of his visit to the scene of the recent carnage, he gathered up two or three unexploded conical shells, not dreaming that there was danger lurking there. He placed them in his wagon and drove away. But, alas! He had not gone far when the jostling of the vehicle over the rough ground brought the shells into contact, and a fearful explosion followed, which resulted in the death of the three persons, and the annihilation of the team and wagon.

Upon another occasion, while standing upon the hillside on this field, in company with comrade David Ritchie, we observed a civilian trudging along with his arms full of shells. Ritchie called to him, saying, "Say, mister, if you knew what those things were you wouldn't be carrying them that way." The countryman replied, "Oh, I know what they are." Just as he was speaking, one of them fell from his arms and went rolling down the hillside. It had gained considerable momentum in its course when it came into contact with a stone. It let loose with a bang that waked the echoes. It was amusing to see with what tenderness that fellow placed the remaining shells on the bosom of Mother Earth, and tiptoed away from them, as if he feared his footfalls might set them off. He let no grass grow under his feet until he had put a safe distance between him and those innocent looking elongated globes.

Soon after the episode of the shells, another of my comrades and myself concluded we would vary the monotony of camp life a little by securing a "pass" and going fishing. We put our plan into operation and proceeded to the river bank and there, James Axton and I made ourselves as comfortable as possible under the circumstances. We had been fairly successful in persuading a number of members of the "finny tribe" to leave the watery element and join our soldier band. This we did by hook and not by crook, of course. But what I was about to tell you was that just opposite where we were doing the fishing act stood a log cabin from which proceeded a woman on horseback and I observed that she headed her horse in the direction of where the rebel army was encamped. It awoke my suspicions, and I called Axton's attention to the fact, but he laughed at my fears, and to show that he had no misgivings as to our security from danger, pulled off his shoes and wading to a rock at some distance from shore, quietly seated himself and proceeded with his fishing.

I, meantime, had gone down the river some two or three hundred yards and was also busily engaged watching for bites, when all at once "biff-bang" from the cabin came a volley aimed at poor Jim on the rock, and the way the bullets made the water fly around that stone was a caution. Jim said he wouldn't have cared so much about their shooting into the water and scaring the fish but he thought they were too careless about their shooting, for some of their bullets tore holes in his clothes. He said they might have accidentally hit him. Sharing Jim's misgivings about the carelessness of their shooting, we both beat a hasty retreat. Leaving fish, shoes and all, we climbed that river bank and took refuge in the bed of a canal, the banks of which had been cut by the rebels for fear it might be of some service to the Union forces. It later fell into Federal hands.

Well, when we found ourselves secure from the fire of the enemy in the old canal bed we concluded to keep an eye on those Johnnies for awhile and see if we could not slip back and secure our shoes and the fish which we had left in our hurry to move. We concluded, after watching for some time, that discretion was the better part of valor. We returned to camp, provoked enough to remember that we had not only failed to secure the coveted mess of fish, but also had been obliged to leave behind our shoes. However, the next day Axton returned for his shoes and strange to say found them where he had left them, and brought them off in triumph, and furthermore, he took his gun with him. By revenge, he aimed and shot at every living thing he could see roundabout that cabin.

I must tell you something in regard to this brave, generous soldier boy, James Axton. His history is both singular and pathetic. His father was a glassblower by avocation, residing at Brownsville, Pennsylvania, where James was born. During the year 1860, work being slack in his hometown, the elder Axton took a trip down the Mississippi River on a coal boat, was taken sick and sent to the Marine Hospital at Memphis, Tennessee, for treatment. The war breaking out about the time of his recovery, he was conscripted and placed for service in the rebel general, Van Dorn's army. On the other hand, Jim, true to the old flag, enlisted in the Union Army. Jim told me how matters stood, and I asked him what he would do in case he met his father on the field of battle. "Why, I would take him prisoner of course," said Jim. His father, after serving for nearly two years in the rebel army, effected his escape and succeeded in making his way to the Union lines, where he at once enlisted in the Union Army. Meanwhile, Jim was taken prisoner by the rebels and sent to Salisbury, North Carolina, where he suffered from starvation, exposure, and nakedness, until reduced to a mere skeleton. With certain death staring him in the face, he appealed to Sergeant James Eberhart as to what he should do. Eberhart was a member of the same company. Axton told him that he had a mind to enlist in the rebel army, and take his chances of making his escape to our lines. He said, "To remain here a few more weeks means death to me." The sergeant said to him, "You must do as you think best." So, after deliberating upon the matter a short time, he concluded to enlist under the Stars and Bars. Jim Axton was a brave and devoted soldier, enduring the hardships of the march and the camp without a murmur. Gallant in battle, scorning death on the sanguinary field, faithful on guard and picket, he was ever wakeful and watchful for his country's honor and safety. He was all this when himself. But he was now starving and naked, weakened in mind and body, with no other hope of escape except through death. The love of life, which is innate in every human being, came in upon him, like an overwhelming flood and carried him before it. He enlisted, taking the oath of allegiance to the Southern Confederacy, believing that the ends justified the means. Whether he died from the effects of his treatment at the hands of the rebels or in trying to escape from service in the Confederate army, none of his friends ever knew. This was the last we ever heard of James Axton.

It will be remembered that the Battle of Antietam was fought on the 17th of September, 1862. The fall rains coming on soon after, many of the dead were literally washed from their shallow graves, and their remains left to fester and decay, exposed to the action of the elements on the very ground which a few short months before their heroic deeds had aided to make historic. Such is the fate of war. After remaining in camp for nearly three months at Antietam, our command, with others, was ordered forward to Fredericksburg, Virginia. We crossed the Potomac at Berlin. On arriving at Belle Plains, I had the honor of being detailed as guard at General Reynold's headquarters. While thus engaged, I made the acquaintance of his cook. He was known by the name of "Ben, the Monkey Turner." He was the slave and personal attendant of the colonel of a South Carolina regiment known as the "Monkey Turners." This command was organized at Charleston, South Carolina, and like many other untried warriors, had indulged in a large amount of boasting as to what they were going to do to the Yankees on the battlefield. Each of them would slay at least five of the Northern "mudsills," that being the euphonious title given by the Southerners to the people of the North, and when that feat of arms was accomplished they were to return to their native city to enjoy a Christmas dinner. They had heard of the Pennsylvania Buck Tails, and they boasted that if they ever got a swipe at that command they would simply wipe them off the face of the earth.

Well, they got that chance at the Second Battle of Bull Run. The Monkey Turners were pitted squarely against the Buck Tails, and the Lord have mercy on their souls, for the Buck Tails with their seven shooting Spencer rifles, almost annihilated the regiment. Ben's master was killed, and as Ben was going onto the field to try to bear off the body of the fallen officer, he chanced to meet three or four of the Monkey Turners running for dear life to the rear. Ben was taken prisoner by the Buck Tails, and General Reynolds installed him as the headquarters cook, where he presided with great dignity. He proved not only to be an efficient cuisine artist, but also an unfailing source of amusement to all who came into contact with him, as he had an exhaustless fund of funny stories locked up in his cranium, from which he was ever able and willing to draw for the entertainment of his friends. While it is impossible for me to accurately put down upon paper the peculiar effect given to a story through the idiom of the African race, I can record how the light of this mirth and laughter reached the hearts of many soldiers, even when the surroundings were gloomy and forbidding.

About this time there were very stringent orders promulgated against foraging, and woe to the fellow taken in the act. He would be escorted to the general's headquarters and caused to stand on the head of a barrel with the stolen property, whatever it might be, placed upon his shoulder. There, under guard, he would be obliged to stand for a longer or shorter time, according to the enormity of the offense, and to be guyed by his comrades. One day one of the boys having a longing for some veal bought a calf from a planter and paid him for it by giving him an order on the quartermaster, taking a receipt from the planter for the same. He boldly led his calf up in front of the general's tent, and there deliberately drawing his sheath-knife, cut its throat. Now the general, who, as is well known was a great stickler for strict discipline, thinking he had caught a forager red-handed in an overt act, called the guard, who placed the man under arrest. But the soldier assured the general that he had purchased the calf, and in proof of his assertion, showed the planter's receipt. That settled it and the soldier was released. The fun was not yet ended, as the next day the planter put in his appearance at the general's tent demanding payment for his calf on the order given him by the soldier. Then there was music in the air, but it was not of a devotional nature either. The calf was eaten and the general could not find the soldier who had tricked him. The case, now out of court, continued to furnish lots of amusement for the boys.

Cyrus Eislie was easily the most wily, crafty and successful bummer and forager in Company G, if not in the entire regiment. He would accumulate anything from sutler checks to mules. I have myself seen him abstract checks from the drawer of the sutler's desk while the sutler was writing on top of it, and then have the unblushing gall to buy goods and pay for them with the stolen checks. On the outskirts of Fredericksburg, while Eislie was roaming around looking for something to "accumulate," he discovered near a house an old goose setting on a nest of eggs in a laudable endeavor to hatch. Sneaking up he grabbed the goose by the neck and started on a dead run for camp. Just at this time a negro woman made her appearance at the door and seeing Eislie and the goose scooting across the field, began to yell. Eislie was soon being pursued by men who were closely behind him. Owing to the resistance of the goose with its powerful wings, Eislie soon discovered he was being overtaken by his pursuers and the outcries of the slave had been heard by a mounted patrol who also joined in the chase. Eislie therefore was compelled to release the goose and he narrowly escaped capture by jumping a nearby fence and taking to the bushes. It was certainly a laughable and excitable goose chase for all those who saw it.

Chapter Seven

FREDERICKSBURG

"Time rolls his ceaseless course; the race of yore,
Who danced our infancy upon their knee,
And told our marvelling boyhood legends store,
Of their strange ventures, happed by land or sea,
How are they blotted from the things that be!
How few, all weak, and withered of their force,
Wait on the verge of dark eternity,
Like stranded wrecks, the tide returning hoarse,
To sweep them from our sight!
Time rolls his ceaseless course."

Who that survives of the Army of the Potomac, that witnessed the night bombardment of Fredericksburg, can ever forget the terrific grandeur of the sight, while our guns were hurling the tokens of Yankee retribution upon the traitorous city, in the shape of shot and shell, where they crashed and fell like the wrath of God on Sodom and Gomorrah. The northern heavens were illumined by the glories of an aurora borealis which shot its lances of purple fire, and spread its banners of flame athwart the sky, rendering the scene one of the most awful sublimity. It surely was a sight which will live in the memory of all who participated in the unavailing fight, until their dying day. To think of all the unrequited valor, and the precious lives which were snuffed out on that bloody field, is truly appalling; for never since the day when arbitrament by the sword was introduced among nations, did men behave more splendidly, or fight more gallantly than did they. Burnside hurled his valorous columns six successive times against the enemy's works, when the first assault demonstrated, beyond a doubt that the enemy's position was impregnable, and yet the holocaust went on, and thousands of patriotic lives were ruthlessly sacrificed to somebody's stupid blundering. And what renders it more obvious that an awful blunder in the order of battle had been made, was the fact that while the frightful carnage was being enacted on Marye's Heights, on the right, the enemy's lines had been pierced. Had the movement been properly supported, instead of a crushing defeat, Fredericksburg would have been a glorious victory for the Union Army. General Meade's command carried the enemy's lines in a gallant charge under the promise of timely support from General Franklin's division, but through some dereliction the promised succor was not forthcoming at the supreme moment, and the position so heroically gained, had to be abandoned. A pathetic and never to be forgotten episode occurred here. In the charge of Meade's Corps, a beloved nephew of the general had fallen, pierced by rebel bullets. His dead body was secured and placed in front of him on his horse. And with his precious burden he followed his decimated columns as they were forced from the field, for lack of the promised aid. He chanced to meet General Wheaton of Franklin's Corps. Meade in an agony of grief and rage at the useless sacrifice of his men, and covered with blood from his nephew's wounds, and with tears streaming from his eyes, drew his sword to kill Wheaton for not moving his column to his support at the proper time. He was only prevented from doing so by the interference of members of his staff. What a dramatic scene. One worthy the brush of a painter, and yet so far as I know, it has not been mentioned by any writer on the field of Fredericksburg.

The gallant Bayard of the cavalry was killed by a shell, and many company and line officers of the reserves were also killed or wounded. Our total loss in this battle was one thousand, eight hundred and forty-two men. My own company was left under the command of the fifth sergeant, and the regiment was left under the command of Captain Lemon. In fact, the flanks of the division were so depleted that the entire command was sent back to Alexandria to be recruited up and reorganized.

Every soldier who participated in the tiresome, enervating and distressing march known as the "Burnside stick-in-the-mud," will remember its hardship, exposure, and suffering until his dying day. From start to finish the windows of heaven were wide open and a cold rain incessantly, day and night, beat upon the heads of the devoted soldiers. The roadway was speedily converted into a quagmire in which the wagons were buried up to their beds and the mules dropped down in their harness and suffocated in the mud. The troops floundered along both sides of the quagmire in mud from ankle to knee deep, their designation being the fords of the Rappahannock, and their design, to flank the rebels out of Fredericksburg. Owing to the severity of the weather, the movement was a complete failure. The order was countermanded before the objective point was reached and the troops were returned to their old camps. The rebels were informed of this fiasco and on the picket jeered and taunted our men over this miserable failure.

The screaming farce, "Burnside stick-in-the-mud," was dramatized from the original performance as given on Burnside by Mr. Bud Gaskell, who was a participant in the first performance. Gaskell being the originator of the play, was also the star actor, and he was a whole troupe in himself in no need of assistance. The literary merits of this work, I am sorry to say, were not of a high order, consisting as they did principally of ejaculations and exclamations of violent disgust, frequently interspersed with a liberal variety of cuss words that were far more expressive than elegant. His wardrobe for a performance while not grand or expensive was at least singular and attractive. It consisted of a battered plug hat and a ragged coat, if he could get them. If not, his uniform as soldier was amply sufficient. His performance was always gratis and therefore popular. With pants rolled high above his army brogans, disclosing his hairy calves, and clothed in his ragged coat with the battered hat set at an acute angle on his unkempt head, he would go floundering through and falling into imaginary mudholes, seemingly scraping and wiping mud from his person. All the while Gaskell swore and uttered exclamations of disgust and at every step emitted a sucking sound exactly imitating the noise made by withdrawing the foot from deep mud. When to this was added his grimaces, contortions and groans it altogether made a scene that was inexpressibly ludicrous and laughable.

Being on patrol duty in Alexandria one day, I saw a crowd gathered at the corner of King and Henry streets and approached to see what was going on. A showman had rented a room and had on exhibition a large anaconda and a blowhard posted at the door was enlarging on the wondrous sights within. "Here's the greatest living anaconda in the world, twenty-seven feet, two inches long, and weighing one hundred pounds! Caught in the wilds of Central Africa by three black natives.

By the kind treatment of his master he has become perfectly docile. You can stick your finger in his mouth and he will not bite you. Step this way, ladies and gentlemen, and see this great living curiosity for the small sum of ten cents!" Directly, Gaskell approached the showman and an animated conversation took place between the two. I found that Gaskell wanted to be admitted to perform with the big snake but the showman refused. Gaskell remarked that he would bust up his old fraud of a show and going over to the opposite corner began to cry in mockery of the showman: "Here's the only living Anna Conder! She was caught running wild in the lowlands of old Virginia by three black niggers! By the kind treatment of her captors she has become perfectly docile. You can kiss her black ebony lips and she will not bite you. Step this way, ladies and gentlemen, and without money and without price see the great Burnside stick-in-the-mud, after which Anna may easily be seen by the audience!" He then began his performance as described, and in a very short time he had an immense motley crowd of whites and negroes collected around him that completely blocked both streets. The showman was left without a single patron and he finally came to Bud and gave him two dollars and a half to go away. Gaskell, after having a good time and investing a portion of his money in "bug juice," returned to camp hilarious.

On reaching Alexandria we were moved out to the east a mile or so and having been supplied with Sibley tents, established camp. These tents were more roomy, commodious and aristocratic than the little dog tents we had so long occupied and from which the boys used to stick their heads and bark like dogs from the kennel. The irrepressible Gaskell was now in his element and soon made his presence known both in city and camp. One day he came to our tent about half drunk and amused himself climbing the center pole and falling to the ground and tripping and pitching headlong over straws. While engaged in his comical performances one of the numerous "demi monde" which infested Alexandria at that time, made her appearance in camp. Gaskell approached her and pulling his flask of whisky gave her a drink and conducting her in front of our tent, induced her to sing the following local song, a parody of "When Johnny Comes Marching Home" -

"In eighteen hundred and sixty-one.
Skewbaul. Skewbaul.
In eighteen hundred and sixty-one.
Skewbaul says I.
In eighteen hundred and sixty-one
This cruel war it was begun,
And we'll all drink stone blind,
Johnny fill up the bowl sir.

We met a misfortune at Bull Run.
Skewbaul. Skewbaul.
We met a misfortune at Bull Run.
Skewbaul says I.
We met a misfortune at Bull Run
And all skeedaddled for Washington,
And we'll all drink stone blind,
Johnny fill up the bowl sir.

The Marshall house it is the spot.
Skewbaul. Skewbaul.
The Marshall house it is the spot.
Skewbaul says I.
The Marshall house it is the spot
Where Colonel Ellsworth he was shot,
And we'll all drink stone blind,
Johnny fill up the bowl sir.

The slave pen it's as cold as ice.
Skewbaul. Skewbaul.
The slave pen it's as cold as ice.
Skewbaul says I.
The slave pen it's as cold as ice,
Get up in the morning full of lice,
And we'll all drink stone blind,
Johnny fill up the bowl sir.

I bought a rooster for fifty cents.
Skewbaul. Skewbaul.

I bought a rooster for fifty cents.
Skewbaul says I.
I bought a rooster for fifty cents
But the cockadoodle flew over the fence,
And we'll all drink stone blind,
Johnny fill up the bowl sir."

After singing this doggerel ditty she stepped into a tent and seizing a tin cup from a shelf, containing almost a half pint of commissary whisky, she drank it down with a gulp. Well, she was simply paralyzed in a short time and the officer of the guard had to call an ambulance and send her off to the slave pen. Gaskell, after tripping up the peddler and securing some apples started in the direction of the colonel's quarters, falling many times on the way over imaginary straws and twigs. A mounted officer, seated on his horse was engaged in an animated conversation with the colonel in front of his tent, when Gaskell slipped up and seating himself on the horse's hock joints under his tail, went to munching his apples amid many comical grimaces and contortions. The colonel and the officer were entirely unaware of the monkey shoe being performed under the horse's tail until a laughing, jeering crowd had collected. When the colonel discovered him, Gaskell scooted without waiting to hear any remarks.

About three miles above our camp was a small lagoon, or bayou, that put into the land from the Potomac, which was much frequented by wild ducks, as were the swamps bordering the river. Several of the comrades had made ineffectual efforts to shoot them with their army rifles but the Springfield was a complete failure for duck killing and they received much for their pains.

Baer, who was much given to self laudation and praise, went to the bayou early one morning, stealthily approached the shore, and seeing several ducks, fired, and by accident killed one of them. He returned to camp with his prize, triumphant and greatly elated over his success. After plucking and nicely dressing it, he placed it in a mess pan ready for cooking and then proceeded to the campfire where a number of the comrades were congregated and began to blow about the accuracy of his aim and his expertness as a hunter. After allowing him to blow for awhile one of the men said it was probably a wooden decoy duck he had shot as he had seen a number of them down there the other day. This riled Baer and he declared that all the other men who had been down there after ducks were chumps and pot-hunters that could not hit a barn door with a rifle, and therefore they were jealous of him. He continued, "I'm going to have duck for breakfast in the morning and you fellows can stand around with watering mouths and get a smell while you see me eat it." Ritchie said, "Baer, if I was you I would not blow so much about that duck. Somebody might pick its bones for you before morning." "Oh," said Baer. "I'm not a bit afraid of that. I would like to see the man in this company that is smart enough to steal that duck." Ritchie said no more and Baer, after placing his precious mess pan at his head, went to bed and to sleep. Marching orders for the next day were issued late that night and Ritchie was detailed to cook the meat and have it ready for issue to the men in the morning. About midnight Ritchie went to the back of Baer's tent and silently raising the canvas reached in and abstracted the duck which was placed upon the fire, cooked to a turn and devoured by himself and a comrade. The bones, after being trimmed, were returned to the mess pan and it was replaced at Baer's head without disturbing his slumbers. Baer upon discovering the loss of his duck, raised a howl that was pitched in an altogether different tone and tune to the song of full self praise he had been singing the previous evening. As the last laugh was on him and Ritchie being decidedly handy with his fists, Baer had to stand the gibes of the entire company. On the march and for days afterward in camp he would be greeted with such ejaculations as, "Who stole Baer's duck?" "Who ate Baer's duck?" and "Baer done swaller dat duck whole, I see de fedders on his upper lip," and "Baer, why doan yo' pick dat duck meat outen yo teef?" This continual nagging became unbearable to Baer, and taking advantage of an order issued by the War Department permitting infantry to reenlist in the cavalry, he joined an arm of that service.

Jeremiah B. Jones and William R. Mitchell were two comrades belonging to Company G, of the Eighth, who were over six feet in height each. They were both naturally waggish and witty and overflowing with good humor. Jerry was long and rather thin of build, while Bill was both long and broad. As a number of us were lounging about the campfire one evening Bill asked, "Jerry, where was you raised?" Jerry answered, "Up in the mountains near the Virginia line." "Oh yes," said Bill. "I have heard of the place. The whole township stands on edge and the boulders stick out the side like the warts on a toad's back." "Where was you raised Bill?" asked Jerry. "On Barren Run, near West Newton," replied Bill. "Oh yes," said Jerry. "The killdeers go running over that district with a knapsack on their backs containing eight days rations with tears of grief and despair falling from their eyes." Bill said, "I hear that stock raisers in your township have to tie the sheep together by the tails and hang over the rocks to pick the grass out of the crevices." "There is no stock on Barren Run," replied Jerry. "They can't raise fodder enough there to feed a sick grasshopper through the winter." Bill said, "The farmers of your township have to shoot the wheat under the stones with shot guns." "Well," replied Jerry. "The farmers of Barren Run have to mow with a razor and rake with a fine tooth comb." "It would no doubt be a healthy place to live in the mountains," said Bill. "Only so many of your people are injured in scraping their shins and killed by breaking their necks falling over the rocks." "Barren Run would also be a healthy place if so many of your people did not die of starvation while searching the barren fields with microscopes and field glasses to find dock and dandelion enough to make a mess of greens." Bill said, "In your township they always take dynamite along with the funerals to blast a hole big enough to hide the corpse in." "And in Barren Run all funerals are accompanied by a carload of manure to throw in the grave to rot the corpse," answered Jerry. The controversy now ended amid the laughter of the hearers, with the honors about equal, the principals retired to their tents. The genial Mitchell bravely and nobly met his death on the bloody battlefield at Fredericksburg, and the cheerful Jones perished in the prison hell at Salisbury. Peace to their ashes.

While our ranks were being recruited at Alexandria, small detachments from the regiment were placed along the line of the Orange and Alexandria railroad for its protection and guarding negroes and teams employed in getting out from the surrounding forests, large quantities of wood for the use of the army, and also timber to be used in the erection of blockhouses. The whole of the country in this part of Virginia was overrun by guerillas, and they were very crafty and active, both day and night, and consequently we were obliged to exercise the utmost vigilance in guard and picket duty, and at best they had us at a disadvantage for they were on their native "heath," and knew perfectly every foot of the ground, and could ride fearlessly, where we were obliged to feel our way. But notwithstanding this fact, we were always able to hold our own with them. Wild game was abundant in the woods of Fairfax County at this time, as it had not been disturbed much since the opening of hostilities, between the sections of the country. Men had been too busy in hunting men to waste their energies on smaller game, hence game birds, turkeys, deer, foxes, rabbits and squirrels, had multiplied exceedingly, but the fellow who had the hardihood to take to the woods in quest of game was quite sure to become himself the quarry before the hunt was ended. But the indomitable Ritchie one day sighted what he supposed were two fine wild turkeys, and being a dead shot, he maneuvered until he got within range, and firing brought one of the coveted birds to the ground, but imagine his chagrin when gathering in his prey he discovered it to be a buzzard only. He seemed to relieve his disgust for that particular kind of game by a flow of language which was remarkable more for energy than elegance, and his daydream of feasting on turkey was dissipated for that time at least.

A very singular incident occurred near camp one morning as a gang of negroes were going to their work in the woods. They came upon a fox lying asleep under a tree, and being confused by its sudden awakening, it dashed into a hollow log which was lying close at hand. The negroes clubbed it to death, and brought it into camp in the evening, cooked and feasted off its carcass. I believe this the first and only instance I ever knew of a crafty "Sir Reynard" being caught napping.

One of the most peculiar and distinctive wild fruits of this section of the United States is the persimmon. They grow in great abundance in most of the southern states, and are very toothsome, especially in the late autumn and winter, when they fall from the trees, and become food both for man and beast. I have gathered them from the snow under the trees, in the month of February, and they were delicious, having passed through a candying process in their own sweet juices. They are very nutritious and the persimmon tree becomes a snare and a delusion to the rabbit, where in winter he resorts to feast upon the fallen fruit and thus he falls an easy prey to the negroes, who are well aware of his weakness for the succulent fruit. The persimmon is utilized to some extent also in the manufacture of an intoxicant known to the natives as persimmon beer. The following was the formula: the fruit is first mixed with wheat bran or middlings, dampened, made into large cakes, or pones, and baked in a Dutch oven, and when desired for use, the pones are placed in a keg or other tight vessel and cold water poured over them, and as soon as fomentation takes place, the beverage is ready for use.

At the station at which we were doing service (I have forgotten the name, however, I think it was the first station out of Alexandria, south on the Orange railroad), we had very comfortable quarters, but as we were obliged to escort to the woods and guard the men composing the timber contingent, we were at first unable to get a warm meal at dinner. But at length we hit upon a scheme which enabled us to overcome this difficulty, and it worked like a charm. This was the device: holes about two feet deep and sufficiently large in circumference to nicely admit a camp kettle, were dug in the clay soil, then the first thing upon arising in the morning a rousing fire was started in and over these holes, and the result would be that by the time we had our breakfasts, the holes in the ground would be hot. So we would just insert our camp kettles (all of which were provided with metallic covers), into the holes in the ground, first having filled the kettles with beans, having a liberal chunk of pickled mess pork smothered in their midst. Then we covered the kettles over, with the hot embers left from the morning fire, and on coming in at noon time, there would be our pork and beans, done to a turn, and these supplemented by hot coffee and hardtack, made a meal fit for a king. At least it would fill the aching void beneath a soldier boy's blouse.

One day while at this we were permitted to see what looked for a time as though it might prove a fearful catastrophe, but really ended in a laughable episode. There was standing on the track at the station a train of flat cars, loaded with wood ready to pull out, when around the curve came thundering a train from Culpepper. This train was made up of boxcars, filled with soldiers, some of whom discovered that a rear end collision was inevitable, and gave the alarm, and of course every fellow was intent on saving his own life, and of course they concluded that to jump was the only way out of a bad scrape. And jump they did, one after another, headlong, from the car doors into the bushes which lined the track. In their flight through the air they resembled a drove of giant frogs leaping from the bank of a mill pond into the water. The trains collided with considerable force, but aside from the scratches the boys received from jumping into the bushes, no one was hurt, and all survived to laugh over their needless alarm. However, soon after this, some two miles beyond our camp, the rebels succeeded in causing a wreck which proved disastrous. These rebels were commanded by a Johnny Bull who had recently come from England, named Rodgers, and had taken service in the rebel army, with the rank of captain. The command had one piece of artillery. This they had placed in a concealed position in the woods. Then they drew the spikes which held the rail in position, and attached a wire to the rail, and carrying the wire to their hiding place in the bush, were ready when the train approached to displace the rail by means of the wire. The train was derailed. Then they opened fire upon the wreck and sent a shot from their cannon crashing through the dome of the engine. Several of the cars also were somewhat shattered by their cannon shots, but the "Yanks" were too many for them. Speedily forming, they charged into the woods, took the cannon, killed the captain and captured or killed all his men.

While our command was engaged in doing this guard duty along the line of railroad, the headquarters of our regiment was still at Alexandria, where we had constructed barracks near the government bakery. This was the largest bakery in the world. It converted into bread five hundred barrels of flour daily. The bread was baked in sheets of sixteen loaves, each loaf weighing sixteen ounces, and one loaf of soft bread, or in lieu thereof, twelve ounces of hardtack was the daily allowance for each man, when on full rations. One hundred thousand loaves were sent daily from this bakery to Culpepper for General Grant's army, and large gangs of negroes were constantly employed in carrying these sheets of bread and packing them in the cars, and although the distance was sixty miles to Culpepper, the bread reached them still warm from the ovens. While lying in barracks near Alexandria, a company mess was organized and our excess rations were placed in a general fund with which to purchase extras for our tables.

A negro cook was employed, and as he was an expert in piscatorial matters, and as all kinds of fish were plentiful and cheap, the baked shad and sturgeon which often graced our tables would have caused the mouth of an epicure to water. As the Yuletide drew near the bakers secured a fine lot of turkeys which were dressed and placed in the pans ready for roasting for their contemplated Christmas dinner, but "the best laid plan of mice and men gang oft agree," and it is safe to say that the bakers dined, on that Christmas day, without turkey, as some of our wide awake boys had seen their way clear to confiscate the birds. And so it turned out that what was the baker's loss was the soldier's gain. But the bakers were wrathful and lodged complaint with the colonel, and he of course ordered an immediate search of the quarters. Lieutenant Ramsey, of our company, was the officer of the day, and not a turkey bone did he discover. And yet, the boys were sure that they ate turkey for dinner that day.

Chapter Eight

DEATH OF SISLER

While lying here the rebel hosts invaded the old Keystone State and the Reserves immediately petitioned Governor Curtin to have them sent to the defense of their native state. Two of the brigades were sent and tackled the Johnnies at Little Round Top, some of the boys fighting in sight of their homes. The other brigade was held at Washington and Alexandria for the defense of those cities in case of rebel attack. Upon General Grant taking command of the Army of the Potomac, the Reserves, having recouped and refilled its ranks, rejoined the army at Culpepper, and participated in all the battles of Grant's subsequent campaigns. The series of battles which followed on Grant's assuming command, have been fully described by able writers, but a few incidents of personal observation during the campaign from Culpepper to Petersburg may be of interest to the general reader.

While the death of a comrade always brought sadness to the hearts of those who survived, yet there seemed something inexpressibly sad in the death of one, who having endured the privations and hardships of the soldier life, until after the expiration of his term of enlistment, when his heart and mind were full of the joyful anticipation of the home-going. I say it seemed more distressing to see such a one fall just upon the eve as it were of his home-going, but how often it so happened, many a surviving comrade can attest. Among my messmates was one, a genial, great-hearted, brave young man whose name was John Sisler. Death had deprived him of both fatherly and motherly care, for at a very early age he was left an orphan. He had found a home and had been carefully reared by a family near Uniontown, Pennsylvania, by the name of Parshall. At Robinson's Farm, on May 8th, 1864, where the field was skirted by a dense piece of woodland, the timber of which was principally of pine, we had improvised a line of rifle pits from which our skirmishers would sally, ever and anon, to feel the strength and position of the enemy. I had observed, not far from our rifle pits, an oak, growing among the pines, which forked at about four or five feet from the ground, forming two trunks. In the rear of our position was an old field wherein had sprung up clumps of bushes, here and there. On our withdrawal from our skirmish line at the margin of the woods, a rebel sharpshooter had located himself in a pine tree and from his perch among the branches amused himself by picking off such officers and men as had occasion to pass through the field. John Sisler and David Ritchie, the latter residing at Connellsville, Pennsylvania, were detailed to go out and kill him if possible. Accordingly they slipped over to the timber and Sisler took shelter behind the oak tree above mentioned, and while looking through the forks of the tree was discovered by the rebel, who fired, his bullet striking Sisler squarely between the eyes, killing him instantly. Ritchie, however, discovered where the rebel was located, and shot at him, but his gun was not of sufficient range to reach him, so he came back and reported the fact, whereupon two of the Buck Tails were dispatched with their Spencers to do the job, and they soon brought Johnnie Reb to terms by shooting him dead from his roost in the pine.

We secured Sisler's body and digging a grave in the rear of the battle line, we sorrowfully laid him to rest, marking his lowly grave with a cracker box lid. Sisler was killed about two weeks after his term of enlistment had expired, but as the companies composing the regiment had entered the command at different dates, the time had been averaged, which resulted in detaining our company, to which Sisler belonged, a few days longer than we were justly entitled to serve, with the result as stated above. Sisler's body was afterwards removed to the National Cemetery at Fredericksburg.

Chapter Nine

INCIDENTS OF THE MARCH

On the march to the North Anna River our rations became exhausted. The commissary wagons were not able to keep up with our marching column, and consequently we suffered from hunger. Observing a farmhouse some two miles from the road in the edge of a wood, myself and three comrades fell out of line and proceeded to it, hoping to get some food. A middle-aged man dressed in a new suit of bluish gray, and two daughters met us at the door. The girls were crying and the three were badly scared at our arrival, but we assured them we would do them no harm and they became quite friendly. One of the girls who had an incipient moustache growing on her upper lip said, "I hope you all won't hurt that tanner over thar." Pointing to a house a mile away, she said, "He's nevah been to the war and says he'll nevah go either." We accused her of being in love with the tanner and she finally acknowledged the soft impeachment and we calmed her fears, telling her we would not disturb her lover. I asked the man if he had any eatables. He said he had twenty-one mouths to feed and they had nothing but some bacon, eggs and milk. I asked him where his twenty-one mouths were and he said he had taken his slaves to Richmond for safety. He also informed me that he had paid one thousand dollars for his new suit in that city and the times had become so desperate that the planters did not know what was to become of them. I told him we were out of food and if he would let us have some bacon and eggs we would pay him a fair price for them. To this he consented and while the girls went after the eggs, my comrade and I accompanied him to the smokehouse where he uncovered a barrel half full of bacon cured from the celebrated variety of hog known as the "razorback," selecting a ham about as big as my two hands placed palm to palm. I gave him a dollar greenback for it and the other boys paid for their eggs. He was so pleased he conducted us to the dairy and gave us all the milk we could drink.

By this time the column had gotten quite a distance away, but we overtook them as they were going into camp on the North Anna. Our artillery was engaged in a lively duel with the rebel batteries at this time, while pontoons were being laid preparatory to crossing the river, so our mess hustled lively to get our bacon and eggs cooked and eaten before a battle commenced. After crossing, the rebels were driven steadily backward until darkness settled over the scene. After the desperate Battle of Spotsylvania had been fought, the regiment's term of service having expired, some were marched to the rear and sent home, while those of us who had "veteranized," were consolidated with the Tenth Reserves. This parting between old comrades of many hard fought battles was pathetic indeed and some boys were moved to tears. Our officers and comrades, our band and beloved flag, were taken away and we were left disheartened and dispirited. Several days elapsed before we regained our noted cheerfulness. In a few days we were on the march for Bethesda Church, with our minds fully occupied by the dangers of the present instead of grief for the past.

We reached Bethesda Church on May the 30th. On this day the term of enlistment for the whole division expired. It had been averaged to fall on this date, as some of the regiments had been mustered into service sooner than others. We formed a line of battle behind a rail fence which ran along the side of a dense wood. To our left was a farmhouse, in front of which was planted a battery of artillery. In our immediate front was a cleared field, in which two negro cabins stood. Beyond the cabins the field was skirted by a heavy pine forest which our battery at the house was vigorously shelling. We had torn down the fence and piled up the rails, and with picks and shovels were busily engaged in throwing earth over them to make rifle pits, when suddenly we heard the rebel yell. On looking to the front we saw a Virginia brigade, commanded by General Ramsey, coming at full charge out of the pine woods. They were making for our battery double quick.

We dropped our spades and grasping our rifles poured a deadly crossfire at close range into their ranks, while the battery rained double-shot grape and canister into them. In less time than it takes to tell it, that rebel brigade was virtually annihilated. Only a very few of them made their escape back into the woods. As I was firing across the top of the pit, a piece of a human jaw containing five teeth struck and stuck upright in a rail just in front of me. I suppose the rebel to whom it had belonged had been hit by a cannon shot and his head had been dashed to pieces. A few yards in front of our position was a slight ravine in which some seven hundred of the enemy who were immediately under fire of our guns had taken refuge. We called out to them, "Johnnies come in out of the rain!" They did not wait for a second invitation, but came at once. One long, lank Virginian, as he stepped over our slight breastworks and saw our shovels, exclaimed, "By God, spades are trump this time!" He was evidently happy at the prospect of becoming a boarder at Uncle Sam's expense for awhile.

After the battle the division marched away to the tune of "Home Again, Home Again, From A Foreign Shore," and the organization known as the Pennsylvania Reserves passed out of existence in the full tide of battle.

Thus the veterans who had reenlisted and the recruits who had joined us, were left on the field without colors, officers or organization. We were soon afterward formed into the One Hundred and Ninetieth and One Hundred and Ninety-First Pennsylvania Volunteers.

While the battle was in progress, I had noticed a rebel soldier with an unusually bright canteen hanging at his side, kneeling behind a stump. Being placed after the battle on a picket detail, I concluded to go and see what Johnnie was doing there. I found that he was dead. His canteen and his body were both literally perforated with bullets. I passed on to the woods from which the rebels had charged, to find the whole intervening space thickly strewn with the dead. My beat extended from the woods to the first of the negro cabins before mentioned. Mine was the last post on the line in that direction. By the time the pickets were posted darkness had set in. Oh, the pitiful cries and groans of the wounded and dying made of that night a night of horrors indeed. But as we had been without rations all that day, when the excitement of battle was over, nature asserted herself, and we were desperately hungry. I began to look about for something with which to satisfy hunger's demands, and directly finding a dead rebel whose haversack seemed to be reasonably well supplied, I cut it off his shoulder. I opened it and in the dark ate what I supposed to be some water-soaked hardtack, but imagine my feelings when in the morning

I discovered that instead of being water-soaked, they were blood-soaked! It was then too late to correct my mistake.

I was obliged to submit to the inevitable. After walking my beat for a half hour or so, the thought occurred to me that it might be well for me to explore the cabin at the end of my beat. Accordingly, I approached and opened the door and walked in, to find housed there twelve rebel soldiers, one captain and eleven privates. To state that I was surprised is drawing it mild. As a matter of fact I was badly scared. I could feel my face blanching and my hair raising, but quickly regaining confidence I exclaimed, as two of them were raising their guns to shoot, "Johnnies, you are inside our lines. You are all prisoners. Everybody stack their arms in the corner." As their captain repeated the order they sullenly obeyed without a word. I then called the corporal of the guard. While waiting for the corporal I talked with the captain who had been shot, the ball passing through the wrist just above the hand. He was a young man, about twenty-one years of age, I judged. He was fine appearing, and very gentlemanly. I asked him if his wound was painful. He replied that it was not, and as at the time it was not bleeding, I had no apprehensions in regard to it. I made him as comfortable as I could and assured him that I would take him to the hospital as soon as I was relieved in the morning, so that he might receive the surgical attention of which he stood in such evident need.

The eleven privates had been taken by the corporal and his guards to a place of safekeeping, and the captain had the cabin all to himself. I left him in seeming comfort, but to my surprise can be better imagined than described when on going to the door to call my prisoner in the morning, I found him cold in death. Reaction had evidently come after the shock caused by the wound, and with it, a hemorrhage in which his young life had ebbed away. It has ever been a source of deep regret to me that I did not think to guard against such an exigency by placing a tourniquet upon his arm. The commander of this rebel brigade (General Ramsey), was killed, falling in close proximity to the other negro cabin, in which were taken ten or twelve rebel prisoners. There was found on the person of the dead general, a fine gold watch, a gold mounted sword, and other valuables, all of which were restored to his friends at the first opportunity, I believe. After being relieved, those of us who had been on picket duty rejoined our respective commands, which had moved back a short distance from the corpse strewn battlefield, near to a commissary, where our hunger-puckered stomachs were soon filled out with an abundant allowance of Uncle Sam's hardtack and "salt hoss."

This battlefield was within six miles of the field at Mechanicsville, where less than two years before the Reserves had crushingly defeated a greatly superior force of the enemy - the end thus being near the beginning. The two thousand of the Reserves that remained of the ten thousand who had fought at Mechanicsville determined that the end of the service of the division should be as glorious as its beginning. From the 1st of May our total loss in the division was one thousand, two hundred and ninety-nine officers and men. One hundred and twenty-four officers, and two thousand and thirty-eight men were all that remained of the thirteen regiments composing the Reserves. One thousand, seven hundred and fifty-nine men reenlisted, leaving about twelve hundred to go home. As those who reenlisted participated in the balance of Grant's campaign, the glorious old Reserve Corps was represented in all the battles of the Army of the Potomac from Drainsville to Appomattox.

After the Battle of Bethesda Church, we were organized as the One Hundred and Ninetieth and One Hundred and Ninety-First Pennsylvania Volunteers, and after General Grant had butted against the impregnable lines of the enemy at Cold Harbor, like Burnside had done at Fredericksburg, and with the same result, he flanked their position. The query naturally arises: Why did he not flank before he butted and thus save the useless sacrifice of thousands of brave, patriotic lives? After the disaster of Col Harbor, which was fought on the same field as was Gaines' Mill, two years previous, with the hostile armies reversed in their positions, we were moved to Seven Pines.

We were formed in line of battle in a wood and were sent into action here to relieve cavalry who had been fighting dismounted, with every fourth man holding the horses. We went in with a hurrah, but the enemy seeing the infantry coming in such enthusiasm and numbers, wisely decided to withdraw, leaving us easy victors on this field. I saw after this battle a remarkable illustration of the wonderful tenacity of human life under conditions which it would be thought impossible for one to survive, even for a single moment. I came upon a rebel soldier who had received a shot in the head, the minieball having entered the skull a little above and in front of the ear, on one side, passing obliquely through and coming out behind the ear on the opposite side. A white slouch hat lay beside him with holes through it, correspondingly exactly with those in the head. A quantity of brain substance had oozed from the wound. While I was standing in wonder that the man still breathed, one of our ambulances was driven up. A doctor stepped out of it, approached the wounded man, raised his head and gave him a drink of whisky. Shortly after taking the potion, the man got up on his feet, walked to the ambulance and unaided, got in and was driven to the hospital. Two things were, I thought, thoroughly demonstrated in this case. First, that man can stand more and severer mutilation than any other animal. And secondly, that commissary whisky must possess great reviving power, as here certainly was the most marvelous display of vitality that I have ever observed in any living thing, unless we consider the snapping turtle. It is said to be able to live for nine days after having its head severed.

This was the last hostile meeting our command had with the enemy on the right bank of the James River. That ground had already been made historic by the battle fought there some two years previously.

Soon after the events narrated in the previous chapter occurred, our command was ferried across the James River and advanced on Petersburg. We encountered the first rebel line some four or five miles from that city. While they had a strong position here, it had a fatal defect as will appear from the following description. They had a finely manned battery planted near a well of water in the corner of a pine wood, which had formerly been used by the people of Petersburg as a picnic ground. Several hundred yards in front of the battery and of the wood, was a well constructed rifle pit which was defended by South Carolina troops. About three hundred yards in front of the rifle pit was a well defined ravine which ran parallel with their line of battle. The sides of the ravine were clothed with a small growth of timber and bushes, while the space between the woods and ravine was clear. So the ravine proved their Jonah, as we entered lower down, out of their range, and marching up until opposite their pits. We were protected from their fire, which passed harmlessly over our heads. Creeping up the bank until we were on a level with the field, we used our bayonets and tin cups in scooping out holes in the light sandy soil, which made excellent protection, and from these "gopher-holes" we were able to pour a continuously hot fire upon their battery and rifle pits. Soon after I had finished my little pit, a major of a Massachusetts regiment ordered me out of it. I replied that I was not in his command. He said that made no difference, that we were overlapping his line and I must get out. Dave Ritchie, a comrade, spoke up and addressing the officer, said, "Who are you, anyhow?" "I am Major Doolittle, sir." "Yes," said Ritchie. "Doolittle, both by name and by nature! Get out of this, damn you, or I will shoot you!" And he got. This was my first experience under fire of explosive bullets and they did crack and snap about us in great order. When one of them came in contact with any hard substance the result was an explosion. One of my comrades, by the name of Samuel Wilcox, was struck in the thigh by one of those bullets at this battle, which exploded on striking the bone, and the fragments tearing out in different directions made six distinct wounds. It is supposed that he died from the effects of this wound, as we never heard from him afterwards. All day the battle raged, until darkness set in, when the firing on both sides ceased. Shortly after darkness had settled over the scene, without a general order, and as if by intuition our line got to their feet. Without firing a shot, we charged simultaneously the rebel works, and rushing over their pits, were among the Johnnies before they knew we were coming. We secured as prisoners the whole batch of them, not a man escaping so far as we knew. The morning following I went over to where their battery had stood on the opening of the battle, and oh, what a sight I saw! It seemed as if the entire human and animal life which had composed its working force had been swept at one fell swoop into the bloody vortex of death. Two of the caissons had been blown up, and among the wreckage were dead men and horses, torn and dismembered, lying thick on the ground. I thence proceeded to the well from whence had erstwhile flowed the life-giving water. It was now choked by the stream of death. In it were the bodies of from eight to ten dead men. Turning from this scene of war's horrible carnage, we moved on to the enemy's main defense line about Petersburg, and took possession of a line of rifle pits which had been abandoned by the rebels when our advance was made.

Here we were directly under the fire of the enemy, and as the men were worn out with fighting and marching, a ration of whisky was issued to each soldier. Being inspired with a sort of false courage, the order having been given to occupy a more advanced position in our front, which by the way was one of great danger, the detail under the influence of a stimulant recklessly exposed themselves to the rebel fire. A number of them lost their lives in consequence.

There were two brothers in the detail, one of whom was killed and his body borne to the rear. The remaining brother rent the air with wailing and lamentations for awhile, then turning, shook his fist fiercely at the rebel line and called down heaven's maledictions upon the murderers of his brother. A man in Company F was shot through the head and though unconscious, lived for several hours. While he was dying, a grave was dug alongside of him into which he was laid as soon as breath left his body. The part of the line upon which we were was near the point at which the rebel fort was mined and afterwards blown up. But about the time the mine was commenced we were moved several miles to the left, where we encamped in the woods and constructed Fort Warren. To our right was a cleared field which was over half a mile wide, and extended clear up to the rebel line. This field was covered with a rank growth of ragweed. The woods on either side of the open space extended flush up to our rifle pits. Stretching obliquely across the field was a strip of oozy, boggy ground, terminating at a spring near the woods on the right, and still another strip of miry ground which terminated in a magnolia swamp at the corner of the woods on the left. This field as well as the woods on both sides, was swept by a terrific fire from the enemy's lines, by both artillery and infantry. It seemed whenever the Johnnies felt like burning powder, this was their objective point, and it appeared to us that they never tired, for they kept it up day and night.

The One Hundred and Ninety-First was commanded by a Colonel Carle who had served as a sergeant in the regular army. He was quite a martinet in his bearing and was greatly given to his cups. He was also overbearing and tyrannical, especially so, when drunk. One day when pretty well boozed he was ordered to relieve a Massachusetts regiment which was in the more advanced rifle pits. In fact, these pits were only a few yards from the enemy's lines. Forming his regiment and riding at the head of the column, with a canteen of whisky swinging from his shoulder, he marched us through the open field in full view of the rebels, up to the rifle pits. The enemy opened upon us a falling artillery fire, under which nine men were killed and wounded before we could reach cover in the rifle pits. Some of the company officers were so indignant at this foolhardy and criminal action on the part of the colonel that they unloosed their swords and refused to serve any longer under him. But in some way he managed to pacify them and succeeded in prevailing upon them to resume their swords. One of the men in the command which we went to relieve, while engaged in laughing at seeing us trying to dodge the rebel shells, got his head above the level of the works, and a cannon shot carried the back part of it away, leaving his features complete, which were still convulsed with laughter. He lay there in death, like a statue of Tragedy, wearing the mask of comedy. But for the overhanging recklessness of our puerile colonel, we should have reached our objective point without the loss of a man. We could easily have done so by a slight detour, on either hand through the woods. That method was thereafter pursued when relieving the line. At this time our fire upon the works of the enemy was incessant, day and night. Our fixed ammunition was brought onto the field in boxes containing one thousand rounds each. The boxes were split open, and the soldiers could help themselves.

    The opposing lines were in such close proximity on some parts of the field, that a conversation with the enemy could be carried on in an ordinary tone of voice, and we finally arranged a truce, the conditions of which were, that in case either side received orders to reopen hostilities, a signal shot must be fired in the air, as a fair warning to the other side. And to the honor of both parties, be it said this stipulation was faithfully carried out. This arrangement was made between the men without the consent or knowledge of the officers. We finally became upon such good terms with each other that traffic sprang up between us. The barter usually was coffee and tobacco. Of the former we frequently had a superabundance, and of the latter they usually had an excess. So the conditions of trade were favorable, and under this treaty we became quite neighborly. Indeed, we sat on top of our rifle pits reading aloud from our northern newspapers for Johnnie's edification, and Johnnie would reciprocate in kind, by reading aloud to us from the papers of his section.

Hearing the criticism that would follow the reading of an article by those of the adverse side furnished lots of amusement for the boys. It was in listening to an article read by a Johnnie, from a southern newspaper, that we first learned of the capture of General Stoneman, who had been raiding with his cavalry in Northern Georgia. At the time the rebs read the article we utterly scouted it, but sure enough in a very few days the account was confirmed by the Northern press.

On the right of our line was a road leading to Petersburg and directly across the road was a fort or rather a strong redoubt, which had been abandoned by our forces evidently from a suspicion that it was being mined by the enemy. I had an opportunity one day, and I took a look into it. The guns had all been removed, and there were oat sacks hanging over the embrasures, but it did really bear traces of counter-mining, however, a fort was built near it on the opposite side of the road. I had been posted as a vidette between the lines for the purpose of watching the movements of the enemy to prevent surprise. I had just been relieved by Comrade Warman when we heard the warning shot which was immediately followed by a volley. We were lying outside our pit, but soon rolled into it, and returned the fire. But finally the fire slackened somewhat, when one of our fellows hallooed across to the Johnnies, "Fire away there you damned rebels! You can't hit anybody!" They ceased shooting in apparent disgust. Our men made a lot of gabions, and ramming them solidly with earth, and getting behind them, rolled them up to where they purposed building a fort, and under cover of the protection commenced digging. This being done during the night the enemy heard them, and opened fire and vigorously shelled them, but with little effect. By daybreak next morning we had a stout embankment, which grew in a short time into a strong redoubt. The lines at this point being so close to each other, it became a favorite spot for desertions. I never knew of but one of our men to attempt it, and it resulted disastrously to him, as he was shot and killed just as he reached the enemy's rifle pits. The shooting was done by one of the Buck Tails.

After being relieved from service on this part of the line, we returned to our old camp. Here the colonel at once proceeded to institute new regulations which consisted of everything being done by tap of drum, and as we had not been schooled in that sort of tactics, it was very awkward business for us. As a consequence, mistakes were frequent. This would exasperate the doughty colonel and he would tyrannically and brutally resent it. Taps were sounded for roll call early in the morning. Upon one occasion some of Company F's men not putting in an appearance as promptly as Colonel Carle thought they should have done, he rushed to their tents and kicked them out. That night several shots were sent whizzing through his tent just over his head, and rushing out he found a coffin at his tent hood, inscribed "Beware," and on it the crossbones. He took the hint and learned the lesson which it took West Pointers sometimes so long to learn, that is, that volunteers are volunteers and not regulars. However, it cured him of his brutal practices and made a pretty decent officer out of him.

The next time we were sent to relieve the picket line it was to the left of where we had been before, and quite near to the magnolia swamp. A number of the Massachusetts men had been killed in this swamp and if I recollect correctly, had not yet been buried.

The rebel vidette post at this point was so close to our pit that the enemy could hear our conversation. It was determined that he should be crowded back further, and as it was my trick on as vidette, I was sent out to occupy his post before he came on for the night. As darkness had not yet settled down, I cautiously crawled out through the ragweed and reached the place undiscovered. After getting my bearings a little, I began looking about me. I saw two Johnnies in bright new uniforms lying outside of their pit. My first impulse was to shoot and I drew a bead on one of them, when it occurred to me that it would be too much akin to deliberate murder. I could not pull the trigger. I have often thought that if "somebody's darling" had realized how near he was to death's door that evening, it would have caused the chills to chase each other up his spinal marrow in rapid succession. I stood my "trick," or rather I should say, crouched it, in the weeds until relieved by Comrade J. Malone. He was afterwards captured and died of starvation at Salisbury. Soon after I was relieved the rebel vidette put in his appearance, and on seeing his post occupied, called out, "Say, Yank! You are on my post!" "I know it, Johnnie," said Malone. "But you can't have it anymore. You're too close to our pit. Here, move back!" And he moved without further protest.

After we had completed the construction of Fort Warren we were moved still farther to the left, and being deployed we covered the line which had been previously held by the Second Corps. This corps had been marched to the rear of the mine, and it was their misfortune to be involved in that blundering and terribly mismanaged fiasco. Myself and a comrade by the name of Williams were placed on picket duty here. Our station was in a strip of pine woods. We remained on this post for sixteen days, relieving each other every four hours, day and night, our food being brought to us. This was a very lonely spot, and the mournful notes of the whippoorwill at night rendered it still more distressingly lonesome. Williams was a long, lean, hungry-looking man, with an inordinate appetite. He would frequently eat his sixteen ounces of bread, meat and beans in proportion, at one meal, washing it down with a quart of strong, black coffee, and like "Oliver Twist" wish for more. He informed me that this voracious appetite was acquired in working as a boatman on the Allegheny River, and that he could easily stow away a small ham, a peck of potatoes, with bread and butter and such other garnishment as might accompany, at one sitting without the slightest inconvenience to himself. But as my rations were more than sufficient to meet my requirements, I cheerfully contributed my surplus stock, which helped to make Williams' stay in the woods more endurable, but I frequently thought that his buzz saw appetite would wreck the oldest boarding house establishment in the realm in a brief time.

From our post in the woods we had a distant view of the mine explosion in front of Petersburg, and a fearful eruption it was. It caused the earth to sway and rock as though riven by an earthquake, while an immense black balloon, a thousand feet or more in diameter, shot into the air a distance of several hundred feet, then bursting, scattered its death dealing fragments far and wide. At least five hundred rebels, with their ordnance and equipment were blown to atoms by the explosion of over ten tons of powder which had been buried beneath the fortress. Had the Federal forces, designated to charge the rebel line after the mine exploded followed the orders given, that day would doubtless have seen Petersburg occupied by the Union Army. But someone high in authority had grievously blundered, as had so frequently been the case on more than one important occasion before in this army. But the soldier, "Not his to reason why. Not his to make reply, but his to do and die."

You will allow me here to say that it is my candid opinion that the history of the armies of the world will be searched in vain for a parallel series of blunders such as typically characterized the Army of the Potomac. They can all be charged to the incompetency of its commanders. As to those made by McClellan, few doubt that they were made on purpose, an outward expression of his inward disloyalty to our country. But what is to be said of the blundering which resulted so disastrously at Fredericksburg, Chancellorsville and Cold Harbor? To say nothing of the abortion of the mine at Petersburg. Can these failures be chargeable to any other cause than that of stupendous blundering? Surely, any one of these catastrophes could have been avoided by the exercise of good judgment and common sense. The superior military ability with which General Lee is accredited was due largely to the blunderings of the commanders of the Army of the Potomac. General Lee made egregious mistakes also, which if they had been taken advantage of by the Union commanders, would have resulted in the utter destruction of the rebel army. Notable among his blunders was the detaching of three whole divisions from his army and sending them to the capture of Harper's Ferry, thus leaving himself with only about thirty-five thousand men, with which to oppose the ninety thousand well armed and well fed men composing George B. McClellan's army. It is evident that General Lee knew with whom he had to deal. General McClellan knew also all about the movement of Lee's forces, as the order for their disposition had fallen into his hands. There can be no shadow of a doubt that McClellan purposely and traitorously withheld the blow which could and would have wiped Lee's army out of existence as a military organization.

The rebels had no braver men or better fighters than had the Federals, and I maintain that there never was a time, from the moment of its organization until its muster out, that the noble old Army of the Potomac could not hold its own against an equal number of Johnnies, or any other soldiers on the face of the earth. The fact remains that the Army of the Potomac was greatly handicapped by the incompetency of its leaders. As a member of that army it makes my blood boil to think how the brave, patriotic men of which the army was composed, had to rest under the suspicion of incompetency. In point of fact, the whole trouble was chargeable to the character of its leadership. They not only blundered themselves, but were incapable of profiting by the mistakes of the enemy against whom they were pitted.

Chapter Ten

THE CAPTURE

As the enemy held the Weldon Railroad, we were marched to Yellow Tavern to seize and destroy the road at that point. Here on the 18th of August, 1864, we advanced upon the enemy's works under a terrific fire from their field batteries, and in the midst of a rain storm. With heaven's artillery let loose upon us, it seemed as though the wrath of God was conspiring with the fury of man, in wreaking vengeance upon our devoted heads. We drove the enemy from their position at the railroad through a piece of woods, and into their line of works, and there succeeded in holding them at bay while the railroad was being destroyed. Our position here being very exposed, every fellow was anxious for his own safety. I succeeded in scooping out a small pit, into which I crawled, but from which I was soon forced to vacate by reason of its filling with water. As the downpour of rain continued, I secured a position behind a nearby tree. While standing behind my tree I saw through an embrasure in the fort a man who was evidently a cannoneer. I aimed, and shot. He fell, and I am glad that that is all I know about the transaction. I do not of course know how all old soldiers feel about such matters. It is, however, probable that no soldier who was in several engagements, and did his duty as a soldier, missed causing the death of one or more of his fellow human beings. While he might have been, and probably was entirely justified in so doing, yet there is an aversion I believe in every old soldier's heart, to knowing that he killed anybody.

At about this time we dispatched Comrade Springer to the rear on a double mission, as our ammunition was nearly exhausted, and we were anxious for a cup of coffee. This little unimportant incident was the beginning of the most desperate and soul-harrowing dilemma we as soldiers were ever fated to be caught in. Springer came rushing back in a few moments with blanched face to inform us that we were completely surrounded, that the enemy was in our rear, and for every man to look out for himself. On hearing this we very naturally started back by the way we had come. I now think if we had taken an oblique direction, to our left, we might have flanked the rebel line and escaped, but that was not to be. We soon encountered a line of rebel skirmishers whom we captured and disarmed. Among our captives was a mounted officer to whom one of our men said, as he threateningly raised his gun, "Get down off that horse, you rebel son of a bitch, or I'll blow your brains out!" The reb dismounted without parley. "Now make off there," says Yank. "I'll do the riding act myself." We started on with our prisoners, thinking we were taking them into our lines, when suddenly we ran into a rebel brigade which was drawn up in line of battle. The tables were turned, the officer so recently dismounted looked up at the man on his horse, and said, "I guess I'll ride that horse again now!" "I guess you will," said the man, and jumping nimbly down, he dashed his gun against a tree. The rest of us imitated his example, thus making our arms useless to the enemy, but as Comrade Mitchell struck his rifle against a tree, it exploded, and I narrowly escaped receiving its contents in my body.

The officer whom we had so unceremoniously dismounted, proved to be the rebel General Mahone, and it was his brigade which now stood so much in our way of escape. It was a startling and remarkable fact, that this entire rebel brigade, in broad daylight, had been marched to the rear of our lines, formed in line of battle and deployed skirmishers without opposition or discovery. In fact, all our line officers had been made prisoners before the rank and file knew that the Johnnies were in the rear at all. Not a shot had been fired until about the time we were engaged in taking the rebel skirmishers prisoners. About that time our batteries opened a hot fire upon us, but they fired too high to do the rebel brigade any harm.

Human language does not contain words sufficiently expressive with which to denounce the criminal stupidity and incompetence of the officer who was responsible for this affair. A simple line of pickets posted on our flank would have rendered such a move impossible upon the part of the rebels, or it would at least have given warning so that the movement could have been checkmated. There were some three thousand of us captured here by the rebels and at least three-fourths of this number were purposely starved to death in the prison hells of the South. We were hurriedly hustled off to Petersburg, the rebels stealing our blankets and the hats off our heads as we were marched along. I had a fight with a Johnnie who tried to take my hat and I managed to retain it, but soon thereafter traded it off for an inferior cap, and a five dollar Confederate note. I swapped, as the Yankee would say, because I realized that it would be a question of a short time when I should be obliged to give it up. They systematically robbed us of everything valuable we possessed.

As we passed through Petersburg, I observed several unexploded two hundred pound shells, which I concluded had been sent in by Uncle Sam as visiting cards. The first night of our captivity found us corralled in the open air near the city. During the night a rebel came among us for the purpose of robbing us of any valuables that might still be found with us. Seeing that Comrade Ritchie still had a blanket, he attempted to steal it, but managed to awaken the wrong passenger. Ritchie jumped to his feet and promptly knocked the rebel down. Upon regaining his feet the infuriated rebel rushed off for his gun. He returned and threatened to kill all the "damned Yankees" in the camp, but a rebel officer, hearing the rumpus, came up at this juncture, and ordered the cowardly cur off the grounds. The following morning we were shipped off to Richmond by rail. On arriving there we were confined in a large brick building, known as Pemberton. It stood on Cary Street, above, and nearly opposite Libby Prison.

While confined in this building John McClosky, who is now living in Fostoria, Ohio, threw a Spencer rifle cartridge which he wished to be rid of out the window. It struck the pavement and exploded. This occurrence caused a great stir among the Johnnies and they at once rushed a number of soldiers and several officers into the building to punish the Yank who had tried to blow up the guard. The Buck Tail explained that having no further use for the cartridge, he had simply thrown it away. This explanation, however, was not accepted and the man was brutally bucked and gagged. After this incident we were moved across to Libby and confined on the second floor of that infamously historical building. The notorious Dick Turner, and his pal John Ross, put in an appearance, ostensibly for the purpose of taking charge for safekeeping of the effects of the prisoners of war. I strongly suspect that it was really for the purpose of wholesale robbery. Turner said to us, "All those of you who voluntarily give up their money and valuables to us, the same will be safely kept and returned to you on your leaving the prison. The clerk will now take your names, make a schedule, carefully describing everything so left with him. But everybody will be searched, and all property not handed over to the clerk will be immediately confiscated." The first division of Turner's speech was a lie, pure and simple, as that prince of thieves, Dick Turner, and his robber gang, never returned, nor ever intended returning anything they had stolen from the prisoners of war.

The latter portion of the speech of the villain we found to be literally true, for they did search everyone of us, and they did confiscate everything that the search developed, including lead pencils, combs, pocket knives, jewelry, watches and money. Indeed, everything but our scant clothing was taken. I happened to have on my person at that time two bank notes, a two dollar greenback and a ten dollar Confederate State note. When I heard Dick Turner's speech, I at once made up my mind to leave as little property with that clerk of his as I conveniently could. Accordingly, I proceeded to cut a small strip of the red leather off of the top of one of my bootlegs, and in this I tightly wrapped my money, and placing it in my mouth I saved it. I also saved my pocket knife, which was a small one, by placing it in the palm of my hand and deftly placed my thumb over it. So I passed the search, and saved my money and pocket knife. This latter article aided me in whiling away many an hour in the prison life which followed that would otherwise have hung heavy on my hands. We would sit for hours and whittle and carve, forming trinkets of wood and bone, some specimens of which I still have in my possession. Shortly after Dick Turner's robbery had been enacted at Libby, we were transferred to Belle Island, which is situated in the James River, above the city of Richmond, Virginia.

The Tredegar Ironworks, then busily at work turning out rebel war material, occupied the upper end of the island while our prison camp, several acres in extent, and surrounded by rifle pits, was located at the lower, or western end of the island. The entrance gate, the cookhouse and the guard's quarters, were on the Richmond side of the island, while an alleyway skirted with tight board fence on either side led to the river on the Manchester side. Through this alley the prisoners passed in getting water from the river. From the alley round to the cookhouse the river made a sharp bend. In this bend out in the river were several small islands, very small, some of them only a few yards in extent. The largest of the group was not more than twenty feet distant from the one on which we were imprisoned, but a deep channel flowed between. These isles were thickly covered with a growth of willows and rushes, and were utilized by some of the prisoners in their attempts at escape.

Lying between the prison pen and the Tredegar Ironworks, was a hill, upon the brow of which was placed a battery whose guns were trained upon our camp. Then across the river, on the Richmond hills, was another battery, with its guns trained in the same suggestive manner. We were supplied with a few old rotten rags of canvas for shelter, but were allowed no fire. And just here I wish to say that in my humble opinion, there existed between the leaders of the Confederate cause, and hell, a league which the Prince of Darkness on the one hand, and Jefferson Davis on the other, stood mutually pledged to carry out in such a way and manner as should best and most fully employ each and all the hell-born devices for the affliction and torment of men. From the middle of the year 1864, until the collapse of the rebellion, I say on, and after, the date last named, were the darkest and most desperate days of the Southern Confederacy.

We search in vain, the whole category of crime, for one, which these desperate rebel leaders would for an instant halt, or hesitate to commit, to bolster their tottering pillars of state. They deliberately planned for arson, with all its concomitant crimes, for the spreading of contagious diseases by means of infected clothing amongst the people of the North, and the wholesale murder, by starvation, of the Union soldiers which the fortunes of war had placed within their power. For shame! For shame! And then to remember that after all this revelry in crime, after all this hellish refinement of cruelty toward our brave, but helpless and defenseless boys, locked as prisoners of war in their dank, reeking prison pens, to be flayed alive with vermin, and finally starved to death by a protracted process. I say then to think that to such as those was extended the executive clemency, and not a villain of them all received the just recompense of reward for their crimes. Oh! How I thank heaven today as I remember and seem to see again, the comrades of my prison life, with emaciated forms, sunken cheeks and eyes, eyes which were want to sparkle and glow with life's loves and ambitions, now glazing in death's slow oncoming tide. I seem to hear again the voice once strong and musical as the spheres, now weak and sepulchral as though it issued from the tomb, as its last cadence dies away in a feeble cry for bread.

As I remember these things my heart swells with gratitude when I remember also that Jehovah hath said, "Vengeance is Mine! I will repay!" Thus saith the Lord. It was not until after the regime of starvation was inaugurated by the rebel government as a course of treatment of the prisoners of war, that the other barbarities which I have enumerated were put into practice, so that those of our comrades who were prisoners during the earlier period of the war scarcely know what breathing holes of hell these later prisons were. Here it was that imprisonment for a few months meant death sure and certain, graduated solely on the power of constitutional endurance of the individual prisoner. May God forgive those worse than red-handed murders if He will, but I believe I never can.

To continue the account and description of our camp on Belle Isle, the space between the water and the bend in the river before alluded to, down to the water's edge, was utilized for the purpose of counting the prisoners. We were turned into this space as often as every other day, and as we were marched back into camp, we were counted off by the rebs. This ground was, when first set apart as a corral for us, well set with grass, but the starving men soon had pulled the last spear of it, and ate it up, root and branch, until that ground was as bare as the rock of Gibraltar. At all times save when the counting process was going on, a heavy guard was maintained along the line of the alley, and also around the camp. But when we were out for the purpose of being counted, at such times they only had a light guard along the river front. They were well assured that no one would be likely to attempt swimming the river, at least, in the daytime, in an effort to escape. One day when they had turned us out for counting a rebel guard posted at the bend, in order to mark the end of his beat, laid down his shelter tent. I had my eye on that tent, and I wanted it, and I concluded to have it, or fail in an attempt to secure it. So I watched the guard until he rounded the bend on his beat, then I gobbled the tent and hustled up into the crowd and gave one-half of it to my comrade. We made short work of wrapping that canvas around our bodies, and, sooth to say, we got safely into camp with it too.

In the course of the day there were seven brave fellows who had determined to make a break for freedom, so, watching until the guard was well around the bend on his beat again, when silently they dropped into the water, and swimming to the isle twenty feet away, they drew themselves up amongst the willows without having been discovered by the guard. Their design was to lie concealed till night came on, then to swim the river and so make their escape. But the rebs in some way discovered them, and they were brought back, and made to ride the wooden horse as a punishment. It was a trestle such as carpenters use to rest lumber on which they wish to saw, only that the wooden horse trestle is longer of leg than that used by the carpenter. Now that is all it takes to make a horse of the kind under discussion, but now as to the fellow who has to ride the horse, I will tell you how they fix him. They take the offender and set him astride of the trestle, tie his hands behind his back, then a tent pin is driven into the ground on either side of the horse. A tent rope is fastened to each of the ankles of the rider, then made fast to the tent pins which are then tightly driven into the ground, and while the rider's feet cannot touch the ground, he is stretched down so closely that he is in no danger of becoming unhorsed. His hands being fastened behind him he cannot protect himself from the swarms of gnats and flies which attack his face and neck. Being totally unable to shift his position, the torture becomes unbearable and the victim often faints away. I saw two of the recaptured prisoners faint, when I walked away from the brutal scene, wishing that I had almighty power for about one minute. If I could have used it, you can well guess to what use I would have put it to. The day following the rebels shaved the verdure off those little isles until they were as bald as goose eggs. There was no more hiding there.

Some days after, when we were turned out for another count, I observed the imprint of a man in the sand, and like Robinson Crusoe on discovering a footprint in the sand, I was startled. It instantly suggested to my mind a method of escape and quickly obliterating the telltale imprint, I walked up to rear of the cookhouse, where I had observed an old Sibley tent pole to be lying for a week or more. I had been cudgeling my brain for a chance to secure and use it, now here was the chance, and the use would come later. I laid hold of it, and after a little struggle I succeeded in wrenching off one of the three iron feet and rolling it up in my shelter tent I carried it into camp. I immediately called a council of war among my messmates, and submitted my plans, which received their approval.

The next time we were turned out for count, a compact ring or circle was to be formed by us, so that the guard could not see what was going on within. Thus screened we were to dig a cave in the sand, of sufficient size to accommodate two men. For digging we used the iron foot I had secured from the tent pole. The men were to be covered up in the sand, and to remain until sometime the following night, when being outside the guard they could swim the river and make their escape, and at the next count off two more, and so on. On our next outing we dug our hole according to our plans and specifications and selecting Comrades David Ritchie and Calvin Darnell, they being small men, we buried them up, leaving holes for air which we concealed by placing some dead grass over them. The next time the hole was to be enlarged, and Isaac Andrew Moore and myself, two of the larger men in the mess were to have our inning. With what anxiety we watched that spot of ground that afternoon. Imagine our alarm when late in the day we saw some pigs rooting around near where our boys were buried. Those infernal swine, they kept poking around there until one of them stepped into one of the breathing holes. Ritchie caught him by the foot. I saw the pig jerking to get loose, and as there were two rebels engaged in fishing only a short distance away, I was fearful lest they would observe it, and enter upon an investigation of the cause of the strange action of the hog, but they did not seem to see it at all, and Ritchie let go of the pig's foot, and he walked off as if nothing had happened. I have often wondered why the rebs kept those pigs in the enclosure about the cookhouse, but after debating the subject to some extent we reached the conclusion that it was to garnish our soup with a pork flavor, as we have oftentimes detected them with their snouts in our soup buckets before the soup was served to us. However, I never was so fortunate as to find a scrap of meat of any kind in my soup, while in

Belle Isle. But I conclude that you also are becoming anxious about the comrades whom we left buried in the sand some hour since.

Well, as the rebel officer of the guard that evening was making his rounds, a soldier belonging to a New York command called him up to the fence and informed him in regard to Ritchie and Darnell, and pointed out to him as nearly as he could, where they were in hiding. The officer drew his sword and proceeded to make search after the hiding prisoners. He pierced the ground all about them, but failing to find them sent word to Major Turner at Richmond, who had charge of all prisoners of war in and about Richmond. Now, while this Turner was no relation to Dick of Libby, they were as near kin in villainies, as two peas in a pod. The major came over to the island armed with an old pepper-box revolver. He had twelve or fifteen soldiers with him. These he set to work jabbing around in the sand, until one of them stuck Ritchie in the head. This caused him to cry out. Then they set about digging the boys out of their hiding place. As soon as poor Ritchie was out of the hole the valorless major presented his revolver to his head and endeavored to shoot him, but the weapon refused to respond. After snapping at it for awhile, he threw it into the river in disgust. He then ordered that the prisoners be kept in the hole where they were found for two days and nights, without food and water. After placing a guard over them, the rebel returned to his post at Richmond.

On our being turned out again for count the next day we threw them some small bits of bread which we had saved for the purpose from our own meagre rations. We could not give them any water. After remaining in the hole for the prescribed length of time, they were allowed to rejoin the mess. The man who informed the guard of the plot of these boys to escape was found out by one of our men, and we were about to organize a court martial for his trial, when we were all shipped to Salisbury, North Carolina. I later learned that he died of starvation.

As food is the all-absorbing thought by day and the theme of dreams by night to starving men, it is proper to give a description of the quality and quantity of the grub, for to call it food would be to misname it, even if it were designed for hogs. It would be almost impossible to give one who did not have an opportunity of seeing the rations which were furnished us, as prisoners of war at our country retreat on Belle Isle, and at the "Hotel de Libby" in the city. For breakfast we had a piece of corn bread about two inches square, or one slice of wheat bread (usually sour), and one pint of coffee (so-called), made from parched rye. For dinner we had absolutely nothing. For supper we were served the same amount of bread, and of the same quality, and either a pint of rye coffee or instead thereof a pint of pea soup, or one tablespoonful of boiled rice, or two ounces of rotten bacon or beef. This constituted the entire bill of fare at the two hostelries named. The variety consisted alone in the fact that if you got coffee you did not get soup, and if you got soup you did not get rice, and if you got rice, you did not get meat. They never made the unpardonable mistake of serving any two of the articles named at any one meal. The peas used in making soup were of a variety known in the South as "nigger peas," and were invariably bug-eaten. The soup was flavored with a bit of the kind of pork of which I have spoken. It was necessary to skim the bugs off before the soup could be swallowed, as they arose to the surface in great quantities. In regard to the bacon furnished, if the human mind can conceive of anything really loathsome, that bacon would stand for its representative. If a bit of the rind were lifted it would reveal a squirming mass of maggots and worms, or if it were cooked, there they would lie in grim and greasy rows, rigid in death. The beef supply consisted of shin bones and heads from which the tongues were invariably extracted, and the eyes left in, and sometimes the cud would be found sticking between the jaws. When the meat was served an ox eye was a full ration of meat for one prisoner, and the poor starved men would trim and gnaw them until they had the appearance of large glass marbles. On Christmas, New Year, and other holidays, we were given nothing whatever to eat.

One day when we were to be counted, I saw a rebel give a prisoner a quart of peas, and surmising that they had been given to him as a reward for informing, I concluded to watch him. I did so. The poor fellow being so near starved gulped them, as a hog might have done, without chewing, but very soon his famished stomach revolted, and he threw them up. Then one of his comrades carefully picked them up from the ground where they had fallen and ate them. Oh, the rarity of Christian charity under the sun! What a commentary upon zealous teaching and preaching. Here was a Christian man starved by Christian men until he was reduced to the miserable extremity of eating vomit like a dog. This systematic and diabolic plan of starving helpless prisoners by our Christian brethren of the South stands unparalleled even by the annals of the most depraved and barbaric savages of any tribe or nation that was known at any time to have polluted and disgraced God's green earth.

The starving of our prisoners of war by the rebels was not, as some apologists would have us believe, an incident of the war, which was brought about by a chance contingency. Far from it. This method of starvation was deliberately planned and adopted by the authorities of the Southern Confederacy as a means to an end. That end was the weakening and reducing of the men composing our army. How well their design succeeded was witnessed by the skeletons of nearly seventy thousand men, literally starved to death in the prison hells of the South. Indeed, there were about twenty thousand more Union soldiers starved to death by the rebels than were slain in battle during the whole course of the war.

The inexplicable policy of our own government in refusing or neglecting to exchange prisoners of war, or to enforce, by retributive treatment, the proper care of those who were unfortunate enough to fall into the rebel's hands, was indeed reprehensible, and was only exceeded by the brutality of the rebs in the execution of their starving policy. It has often been said that the rebels really did the best they could to provide their prisoners with food and care, but that they could do no better for lack of money. This is untrue. There was never a time during the whole course of the war that the rebels could not have fed their prisoners plentifully had they so desired.

There is not a case on record of a rebel soldier starving to death, and yet these perjurers swear that Union prisoners were fed the same quality and quantity of food as were their own soldiers. Clothing and canned food were sent in large quantities from the North for our use, and were stored in a building within sight of Belle Isle, yet not a jot nor a tittle of them ever reached us. After the rebels had stolen what they wished of them, the torch was applied, and the balance burned. This was not done until Richmond was evacuated, which proved conclusively that the starving of the prisoners was deliberately designed. Had our government retaliated by feeding the rebel prisoners who fell into our hands in the same manner, there never would have been a case of a starvation reported from any of the prison pens of the South.

This action on the part of General Grant, who had supreme command of all the armies of the United States, preferring to allow our comrades to starve and die by the thousands rather than chance the meeting of the exchanged Confederates in the field, is a sad blot on his otherwise famous record.

Chapter Eleven

THE FIRST ESCAPE

On the 6th day of October, 1864, one thousand and three hundred prisoners, were provided with what the rebels informed us were three day's rations. These paltry rations were all consumed at one meal by most of the men. I distinctly remember what an exertion of will power it cost me to even save a small piece of corn bread from my allowance. We were loaded into boxcars and started for another rebel starvation hell, located at Salisbury, North Carolina.

Sixty-five men were crowded into each car which rendered it impossible for us either to sit or lie down, so we were obliged to stand like cattle in a stock train. The doors on the right hand side of the cars were locked, while those on the left were open. There were two guards stationed in each, and a number of guards also rode on the deck of each car. The cars were old rotten-looking things, and when the train once got underway it rattled and banged in a way to drown all other sounds. I set about kicking at the front end of the car in which I was riding, and I soon succeeded in breaking a hole through it large enough to crawl out of if the opportunity came. So, giving one-half of my dog tent to my comrade, Isaac Mitchell, I told him that the first stop the train made I proposed to make a break for liberty. He said, "I will follow you." The first stop which the train made was for wood. So out I crawled, onto the bumpers, and down to the ground between the cars and out onto the side where the guards were standing in the doors.

I started boldly alongside the train toward the engine. One of the guards in the car next to the one I had escaped from as I passed, cried, "Halt, who goes dar?" Without stopping, I turned my head and said, "Who the devil are you talking to!" I then passed without further challenge, it being so dark they could not distinguish the color of my clothing. Mitchell, who was partly out of the car on hearing them challenge me, drew back, so I was thus left along. Going up to the engine, where a gang of slaves were throwing wood onto the tank, I soon put the woodpile between myself and the cars. Stepping behind a large tree, I waited until the train had pulled out and the men had gone. At about this stage of the game every white man, woman and child acted as spies for the Southern Confederacy, and whenever a strange face was seen in a community, it excited suspicion and the stranger was called to an immediate reckoning. I was fully aware of this fact, and had it confirmed through a bitter experience later on. Being alone, and having no one with whom to counsel, I carefully considered my desperate condition, and pondered the best course to pursue in effecting my escape. I was in the enemy's country, south of Richmond, with the rebel army between me and freedom. I was weak from starvation, without food and with insufficient clothing to keep me comfortable during the frosty nights. I had no means of lighting a fire and I dared not show myself to ask for food. My case was indeed a desperate one, and I resolved to adopt desperate means in trying to reach the shelter of the old flag once more. I was already twenty miles and more south of Richmond. I planned to go still further south, and thereby either flank the right of the rebel army, or take the desperate chance of running their lines. I resolved to trust no one, not even the slaves, in fear of betrayal, and yet there I was in a country, the topography of which I was in perfect ignorance. I resolved also to travel both by day and night, and thus make the best possible time, and I further resolved to use every means, however desperate, short of murder itself, in accomplishing my escape.

In looking back on these foolish resolves and plans of mine, the things which to me, in my physical weakness seemed so feasible and easy of accomplishment, at this distance assume the aspect of impossibility. Indeed, when thinking of them in the light of my surroundings, they appear to me like the vagaries of an idiot. The gravest of all my mistakes was not trusting my case to the hands of the negro slaves, who would doubtless have guided, fed and concealed me until I reached the Union lines. But having resolved my course, I left my hiding place, returned to the railroad track and started in the direction which the train from which I had escaped had gone.

I soon came to a field of corn, alongside the track, which I entered and shelled two ears. I ate with great avidity, notwithstanding that I had eaten the elaborate three day's rations with which the rebels had furnished us. After filling my pockets with corn for future use, I continued my journey until about midnight, when I discovered a fire burning on the bank of a stream, which I rightly guessed to be the Appomattox River. The railroad crossed the river at this point on a trestle bridge, and there was a fort on the farther bank. A guard walked back and forth over the bridge while a fire which was located between the fort and the bridge, threw a lurid light for a considerable distance over all surrounding objects. Approaching as near as possible without being observed, I waited until the guard had turned to walk toward the opposite side. Then hurrying to the end of the bridge, I got onto the trestles underneath without being detected, and crawling from trestle to trestle, while the guard walked overhead, at length I reached the abutment on the other side. I found to my dismay that it stood in the water and was about thirty feet high, and that there was no possible way of getting around it. If I were to climb to the top of the bridge I should be in the full glare of the firelight, and readily seen by the sentinel, so there was nothing left me but to make my way back to the side whence I had come. This I did in safety, and circling to the left I hid myself in a swamp, designing to swim the river at daylight. Being tired and worn out I fell asleep and did not awaken until the sun was two hours high. Then after eating some corn I started for the river but did not reach it until about noon on account of its being a crooked, winding stream. I then lost my direction on it.

In my tramp from the swamp to the river I found a persimmon tree loaded with half-ripe fruit. Not being able to resist the temptation I ate of it until my mouth was puckered so that I could whistle a great deal easier than I could sing. Reaching the river I stripped, and tying my clothing in a bundle, tied it to my head and swam the river. While engaged in dressing I heard voices in the distance, which I located as coming from a plowed field lying in the direction I wished to go. Observing that a bushy ravine ran nearly across this field, I entered it and made my way to the end of it, which brought me opposite to a tobacco barn which stood at the edge of a wood. The voices I had heard were those of some negroes who were engaged in sowing wheat at the upper end of the field which was quite a distance away. Watching my chance I got into the barn, which was empty, but I discovered several dinner buckets sitting about and a rebel jacket hanging from a peg. I hastily explored the dinner pails in hope of finding something to eat, but in this I was disappointed. They were all empty, but fastening to that jacket I made off into the woods where I took off my blue blouse and put on the rebel jacket. I tied my blouse up in my handkerchief and travelled. Soon after I struck the railroad track which I followed to the south again, and on coming to a house I sneaked into the garden nearby and pulled a number of very small turnips which I found to be so hot that I could not eat them. Resuming my journey I passed through a little hamlet called Amelia Court House. This was sometime during the night, and going on a little way I turned into a clump of bushes and slept for a few hours. But I had made a mistake again.

I should have turned to the north at the courthouse, but failed to do so. Keeping to the railroad I came to a ramshackle village of a few houses and sheds called Jetersville. It was here where General Lee's wagon train was captured later on. Seeing a wagon road which ran through the rear portion of the town, I took it, as I thought that the safe way, and I succeeded in passing through all right. Immediately beyond the village the road ascended quite a hill and between this road and the railroad was an open pine wood through which I designed to pass and thus reach the railroad track again. But, alas! An arbiter of my fate was ascending that hill, on the other side, unbeknown to me.

As I reached the foot of the hill and entered the woods, I saw two men heave into view on top of the eminence, one of whom was in a buggy, the other mounted on a horse. The horseman dashed down upon me and with drawn revolver ordered me to surrender, which I did, and he marched me up to the party in the buggy, who proved to be the Sheriff of Amelia County. The cavalier was a conscript officer and they were out for human game, and I was it. The sheriff subjected me to a rigid questioning to which I responded with a promptitude worthy of a better cause. I said I belonged to a North Carolina regiment, that my mother was sick, and that I had been given a furlough to go to see her. I told them that I had lost this document and spoke a whole lot of lies which would have made the father of lies turn green with envy to have been able to imitate. But it was no go. That mullet-headed sheriff would not believe a word of the whole lot. He said I was no doubt an escaped Yankee, and he would be obliged to take me back and place me in jail at Amelia. My corn and persimmon diet had left me in such a famished condition that I did not care much where he took me so long as there was something to eat. I demanded food, and he said he would provide supper for me at his home, which was on the way to Amelia.

Soon after arriving at his house the sheriff ordered supper, which was shortly on the table and consisted of corn cakes, fried bacon and sorghum molasses. The facility with which I hid that grub from view caused the wench who baked the cakes to hustle, and the sheriff to conclude that he had captured a gormandizer. While I was at supper, the wife of the sheriff was busy examining my bundle, which I had left in another room. I found the contents of my pack very much disarranged and the sheriff more confirmed in his belief that I was an escaped Yank. But he seemed a very humane sort of a man, and inclined to give me the benefit of any doubts he might entertain in regard to my loyalty to the South. But of course I could not prove my claim.

After supper the buggy was brought out again and we got in and drove to Amelia Court House. On arriving there the sheriff concluded to send me on to Richmond instead of placing me in jail at the courthouse, so he took me to the depot. While waiting for the train a number of rebels, both young and old, fired questions at me, which I answered to the best of my ability. Finally, a man came in and said he was the Major of the First North Carolina Regiment. Now this was the command I had told the sheriff I was a member of, so you can guess I felt sort of streaked. Well, the major said he had been desperately wounded, and was home while his wound was healing, and he proceeded to question me. I was wary and cautious, believing all the while that he was a liar, as well as myself, for I reasoned that if he was a North Carolinian, how did it come that his home was here in Virginia? Finally he asked, "Who is colonel of the First North Carolina?" "Colonel Anderson," said I. "Now by God you lie," said the major. "Colonel Hawkins commands that regiment, and you are nothing but a damned Yankee." "Damn it," said I. "You have not seen the regiment for over a year and how do you know what changes have taken place in that time. And I believe that you lie also, for if you belong to the First North Carolina, how does it come that I find you living here in Virginia?" I knew that the rebels brigaded their men from the different states by themselves. The sheriff laughed heartily and this answer shut him up, but another of them said, "Well I know you are a Yankee anyhow." "And how do you know it?" said I. "Why, you would git as mad as hell when the major called you a Yankee if you hadn't been one," he said. I answered that fellow with a contemptuous look, and mentally resolved that the next time I was called a damned Yankee when I was honestly trying to pose as a rebel, I would "git as mad as hell."

Shortly after this questioning, a train pulled in and I was handed over to the tender mercies of a sergeant by the sheriff, who told him that I was an escaped Yankee, and that he should hand me over to the proper official at Richmond. The sergeant took me into the forward coach and put me in among a lot of rebel deserters whom he was taking to the city under a strong guard. This car had been formerly used as a baggage car, with a door at either end, and wide side doors in the center, but it had been fitted up with seats and transformed into a sort of passenger coach. The sergeant appreciating the desperate character of the Yankee whom he had in charge, selected a trustworthy rebel whose special commission was to carefully guard me, and right royally did he attend to his duty. He sat on the same seat with me and acted as my twin automaton. When I got up, he got up. When I walked the car for exercise, he walked too. When I sat down, he sat down also. Under the seat was the knapsack of my guard, and the car being badly lighted, I took advantage of it to slip my hand down between my knees, and lifting the flap of said knapsack, I pilfered from a rebel vest three pocket handkerchiefs, which I succeeded in placing under the breast of my jacket, unobserved by my attendant who was sitting at my side. The handkerchiefs were marked with the name "Canon," on the corners in indelible ink. I kept one of these for many years as a souvenir of that night's experience. The other two were disposed of as will be related later on. Now, after the lapse of nearly a third of a century, I will say, that if Mr. Canon will make himself known I will cheerfully make him full restitution and apology, and further, in order to emphasize fraternity between the Blue and the Gray, I will set up a supper a la Hotel de Libby.

On arriving at Richmond, and while the sergeant was marching his deserters out of the left side door onto the platform, at the depot, my guard turned his back to me while buckling on his cartridge box. Instantly jumping from the opposite door, I ran up among the cars in the yard until I reached a street. Here I paused a moment to see whether I was being pursued. I was not followed so I hastily put on the rebel vest and tied my blue one up in my bundle. My uniform was now half reb, and going out onto the street, I hastily decided to try to make my way to Fredericksburg, as I was more familiar with the country about that place. While pondering over the uncertainties of my chances of ultimate escape, I was brought to a sudden halt in seeing Castle Thunder and Libby Prison looming up before me in all their grim majesty. I realized now that I was on Cary Street. I hurriedly crossed over by way of a side street to Broad, and boldly started up through the very heart of the city on this street to reach the Fredericksburg depot. On reaching the market house I saw a policeman engaged in lighting a gas. I approached him and asked the way to the depot. He answered me that it was three miles directly up Broad Street. I then continued my way until I came to the Central Depot, and knowing that just twenty-three miles out, at Hanover Junction, this Central Railroad crossed the one leading into Fredericksburg, and I feared that if I continued this direct course to that point, I'd be pulled in. I decided to set out along the line of the Central Road. After getting out about three miles from the city limits, I observed a man who seemed to be drunk staggering along ahead of me. Thinking that I would be able to hold my own with him even should he prove hostile, I quickened my steps and soon overtook him. As I was passing him he said, "By God ole feller, you are going to run the blockade tonight!"

This greeting somewhat alarmed me, but I replied, "Oh, I guess not." "Yes, you are," said he. He then added, "If I only had my shirts here I'd go along with you." These words relieved my fears and I admitted that it was my intention to run the lines if I could. We then sat down and talked awhile, and I tried to induce him to go with me, but could not do so. He said everything he possessed in the world was in camp, and he said he would be arrested on his return to camp as he had been on a protracted drunk in Richmond and had stayed too long. His name was Frank Hardy, and he was Irish by birth. He said he was sick and tired of the rebellion, and would desert at the first opportunity. He was a member of Company C, Nineteenth Virginia Battalion. His captain's name was Hetherington, and his colonel's name was Anderson. He said that they were in camp at Mechanicsville, engaged in guarding the line of the Chickahominy. He also told me how the guard was posted at the bridge at the crossing of the stream. And he requested that if I got through to go to a man by the name of Spofford who kept a saloon in Alexandria, and tell him that Hardy was going to run the blockade at the first opportunity. He then gave me his pass, saying that it might be of use to me, and shaking my hand, wished me success in my perilous undertaking, and bade me goodbye.

The pass given me by Hardy was dated Richmond, October 5th, 1864, and read as follows: "Frank Hardy will immediately rejoin his regiment on the Mechanicsville road." It was signed by Brigadier General Gardner, commanding at Richmond, Virginia. I have not been in Alexandria since meeting Hardy and so I never delivered his message to Spofford. Neither have I learned whether he rejoined his regiment as he was directed to do in the pass, nor whether the opportunity for running the blockade, as he called it, ever came to him. Of one thing I am sure, however, that if Frank Hardy is still in the land of the living, even at this late day, I would be glad to hear from or see him.

Soon after parting from Hardy I came to a field of standing sorghum cane. I cut a stalk of it and chewing it, swallowed the juice which constituted my supper. Taking more of the cane, I placed in under my arm for future use and proceeded on my way rejoicing. And reaching the Chickahominy, I crossed over on the railroad bridge without encountering a guard. I found a clump of bushes just beyond which seemed to offer reasonable seclusion. I crept in and being very weary I soon fell asleep, but on awakening I was chilled to the bone, and was obliged to resume my tramp to get my thinned blood into circulation again. As I plodded along I was wishing I could get hold of some matches so I could fire the bridges and the wood which were ranked along the railroad on which I was travelling, not stopping to think for one moment that such a course would result in my certain and speedy capture, and that if captured, with such a charge of vandalism lodging against me, I would have been hung higher than Haman, without judge or jury. That such an idea should ever have entered the head of a sane person is past all comprehension, and then to think that I was deterred from such a foolhardy enterprise by the merest accident, causes me to shudder.

On Sunday morning, October 9th, and the fourth day after escaping from the boxcar, at about the noon hour I came to a large clear space, and looking about me, I discerned a fort and I at once concluded that I was in close proximity to the South Anna River. Prudence at once suggested that my safety lay in hiding until night came on, but my famished condition and my overwhelming desire to reach the Union lines urged me forward and lured me on to my undoing.

Leaving the railroad, I took across the fields so as to strike the river about a mile below the fort, but as I reached the brink of the stream, two rebels rose from behind the bank and aiming their rifles at me called upon me to surrender. There was nothing else to do but respond to the demand with the best grace possible. I had been seen from the fort and these two soldiers had been dispatched to intercept me. I was marched up to the fort and taken before the captain commanding for examination. This officer was a venerable appearing, gray-headed man, of about sixty-five summers. His company belonged to a reserve corps and was composed largely of old men and young boys. I still held the pass given to me by Hardy. Showing it to the captain, I tried to have him think it read Fredericksburg instead of Mechanicsville, but had no success. He said his orders were very strict in regard to letting anyone pass this point, and that even if my pass had read Fredericksburg he could not honor it. The time limit had expired several days ago on all passes beyond this point. He would be obliged to send me on to Richmond.

As I had eaten nothing but raw corn and unripe persimmons since I supped with the sheriff and was famishing for food, I asked the captain for something to eat. He answered in a surly manner that he had nothing for me, but called up an old man of about sixty years of age and a boy of fourteen or fifteen years, and ordered them to take me to a fire which was burning in a corner of the fort. They would keep watch over me until the train came along. In taking me over to the fire, the boy, who no doubt had an exalted opinion of his own importance, strutted along close to my side very much like a young fighting cock would. I said to him, "You need not be so particular to keep close to me. I'm not going to run away." Patting the old Harper's Ferry musket with which he was armed, he said, "By God, I know you'll not run while I've got this gun, 'cause I believe you's a damned Yankee, anyhow." Remembering my promise to get as mad as hell when the next fellow called me a Yankee, I said, "See here, young fellow, if you hadn't that gun I'd smash your nose all over your face. I'd teach you to call me a damned Yankee!" The old man said to the youngster, "Shut up, God damn you. He might be as good a soldier as you and a damn sight better, too." This effectively squelched the young warrior and he had nothing more to say to me.

I then asked the old man for something to eat, and he answered that they had nothing. I told him that I'd had nothing to eat for two days, and that I knew they had something that would satisfy hunger, for they could not stay there without food. He then brought me a piece of bacon and two large sweet potatoes, and I soon had those potatoes in the hot ashes and the meat toasting on a stick. About the time I had finished my meal the train came in sight, and the captain sent a man to flag it to stop. I then asked him to return me my pass. He said, "I will send it to Richmond." I said, "You are sending me there and I can take it. It belongs to me and I want it." He then gave me the pass, and put me on the front car of the train, telling the conductor that I was an escaped Yankee.

Now in the rear car of this train they had thirty-two enlisted men and two officers who had been captured from some Pennsylvania regiment. They had been taken at Salem, in the valley by Mosby. I think these prisoners belonged to the One Hundred and Sixteenth Pennsylvania Volunteers, and they were being taken to Libby. In charge was a rebel captain supported by ample guards. The conductor took me back through the train, and opening the door of the rear car put me in among the Yankees, and neglected to tell the officer in charge that I was an escaped Yank. I took a seat beside one of the Yankees without speaking to anyone, but I was sure doing a whole lot of thinking. I had very soon formulated a plan, somewhat desperate and dangerous, I concede, but I had worked myself up to the required pitch for desperate undertakings. And now it became necessary for me to play the role of injured innocence, so I boldly approached the rebel officer and said, "Captain, see here, I'm no Yankee, and I don't want to sit on the same seat with a damned Yankee. This will tell you who I am." I handed him the pass. He read it, and turning to me, said, "Well, sit down on the seat there with the guard." Observing that the officer did not seem to question the legality of the pass, I said, "Captain, I am very anxious to join my company. I wish you would take me to the Provost Marshall and have me sent to the soldier's retreat, so that I can get back to my command as soon as possible." He said, "All right, I will fix it as soon as we get to Richmond." So I sat beside the guard until Richmond was reached, and on getting off the train the captain asked me to walk down to Libby with him, where he was to deliver his prisoners. He would then go with me to see the Provost Marshall.

As we walked along on our way to Libby, the captain very kindly pointed out to me several places of interest, among which, I remember, was the State House, Jeff Davis' residence, the Spotswood Hotel, as well as several other places of interest, all of which were described by him with apparent pleasure. While I was walking on the sidewalk with the captain, and holding this talk with him, the poor prisoners of war were being marched down through the middle of the street, followed by a mob of urchins who were yelling and shouting after them, and calling them "Blue-bellied Yankees." They yelled other euphonious names at them and threw mud. We finally reached the notorious prison and while the newly arrived prisoners were being counted off I went into the prison office and warmed myself at the stove. When the poor fellows had been counted off they were thrust into a living hell. The captain took his receipt for them from the prison authorities, and we started for the Provost Marshall's office.

I was now about to "beard the lion in his den," but I did this with a settled conviction, that whether I succeeded or failed in passing examination before the provost it was all one. I was dead sure of detection in the end, for if I went to the soldier's retreat and passed there I would be discovered as a bogus Frank Hardy on being taken to

Company C, Nineteenth Virginia Battalion. The officers of that organization would know that I never belonged to them. And the most serious aspect of the whole case lay in this, that if I failed to satisfy the provost that I was a rebel soldier, I would be caught in the very act of masquerading about the streets of Richmond, the capital of the Southern Confederacy, in a rebel uniform. In either case, I was sure of imprisonment in Castle Thunder, a trial by court martial, and probably on the charge of being a spy. These desperately hazardous risks had been taken solely that I might obtain food, for I could have easily escaped from the captain at any time after our arrival in Richmond. My previous sufferings from starvation and exposure had been terrible, and only an iron constitution, toughened by the active, outdoor life of a soldier, could have enabled me to endure it as long as I had. When I considered that both food and assistance could have been secured from the negroes for the asking, and that, too, without risk, I can only wonder at my stupidity.

Well, after quite a long walk we brought up at the Provost Marshall's office and entered. I was, as may easily be imagined, in no happy frame of mind. The captain transacted some business and talked with the provost for awhile, and withdrawing left me to the tender mercies of that boss inquisitor of the Southern Confederacy. Calling me up to his desk the following questions were propounded and answered: "What is your name?" "Frank Hardy." "Where do you belong?" "Company C, Nineteenth Virginia Battalion." "Who is your colonel?" "Colonel Anderson." "Who is your captain?" "Captain Hetherington." "Where are you stationed?" "At Mechanicsville." "Where were you going?" "To Hanover Junction." "What were you going there for?" "To see my wife and children." "How long since you have seen them?" "I have not seen them for six months." "Well, why did you not rejoin your regiment on this pass?" "I got on a drunk, sir, and overstayed my time." "That will do," said the provost, and calling a clerk told him to make an order for the soldier's retreat, and go show me where it was.

The clerk wrote out the order, and calling to a North Carolinian who was sitting in the office, and who was destined for the same place, he started with me for the retreat. The clerk and I laughed heartily at his awkwardness, which seemed to have the effect of putting the clerk into great good humor, and he talked pleasantly as we walked along. Just as we reached the retreat he said, "By God, old fellow, I expected to see you go to Castle Thunder, for it is not often that a man gets off as easy as you did." I replied that I considered myself lucky, and was very glad I had gotten off so easily.

On arriving at the Richmond Hotel, as rebels who were confined there called the retreat, the Johnnies began calling out, "Fresh fish, fresh fish!" "New arrivals at the Richmond Hotel!" Without paying any attention to their jeers, I went upstairs and took quarters on the second floor under a gas jet. The Carolinian stopped on the first floor. The retreat was a large three-story building, and like Libby, had formerly been a tobacco storehouse. It was closely guarded, the authorities no doubt being suspicious of its inmates. Having arrived too late for supper I lay down under the gas jet and went to sleep. About one o'clock a.m., I was awakened by the shuffling of feet and excited human voices, and was surprised to find a lot of rebels surrounding me. They proved to be North Carolina Tar-heels, just out of the woods, and conscripts from that state. They had never before seen gas burning, and they would blow it out and relight it, and feel the pipe to see if it were hot, and then give expression to their astonishment to each other. As I had put up at this "hotel" for the express purpose of securing grub, I waited until they were all asleep, then I proceeded to search several of their knapsacks and haversacks for food. I found each knapsack contained five or six plugs of tobacco and nothing else, while their haversacks were filled with cornmeal only. So, I was effectively balked in my design to steal food from that crowd, and it was evident that they were about as much in need of food as I was.

The next morning the Tar-heels wanted hoecake, and they wanted it badly, but had no way of baking it. I was the proprietor of a saucer-shaped half of a canteen, which I concealed inside my pants by suspending it by a string from a suspender button. I was not slow to discover that I was a monopolist. I was the sole owner of the only bake-pan in or about that ranch, and I proceeded to work my special privileges for all there was in them. I would rent my bake-pan at a stipulated price, payable only in hoecakes. I suspect that the tax I levied upon those Tar-heels for the use of my baker would be classed by latter-day statesmen as high-tariff. Anyhow, I did a rattling business for a short time, storing my revenue in my bundle for future exigencies. But after awhile breakfast was called, and that burst my short-lived monopoly all to pieces.

The men to be fed were formed in open rank, and a negro, bearing a tray of bread, marched down the line and as he passed each man would reach in and take a piece. Even meat was served in this manner. A half loaf of bread was served to each man, with other food in proportion, at every meal. The food was clean and of good quality, and of sufficient quantity. No man would starve or even suffer hunger on such food. There were no beef-heads, no buggy peas, nor rotten bacon served here. With prisoners of war a loaf was divided among four men twice a day, while here a loaf was served to two men three times a day. I had now had practical experience, which proved beyond question that the food served to the rebel soldiers was more than four times as much in quantity and far better in quality than was given to the prisoners. All rebel asservations and affidavits that contradict these statements, are willful lies and rank perjuries. After I became familiar with the mode of distributing food here I fared sumptuously. I would fall into line at the head of the column at the stair landing. Taking my piece of bread I would frequently run behind the line to the foot of the column, and take another piece, thus securing double rations. By this means I kept fairly well supplied.

I was here in personal contact with rebels from all portions of the Confederacy, moved among and talked with them, free from any suspicion on their part. While the great majority of them were densely ignorant, there were some who were intelligent and well posted on the current topics of the day. I learned that it was the universal opinion of the rank and file of the rebel army that should General George B. McClellan be elected President of the United States at the then ensuing election, that England would at once recognize the independence of the Confederacy and the war would be over. Should Lincoln be reelected it meant a continuation of the struggle, with very little chance for their final success, as they said their resources were about exhausted. They also said that McClellan had been the best quartermaster they had ever had, as he had furnished them with supplies which they could not otherwise have obtained.

Amongst the rebels in this room was a young Marylander, a man of fine appearance and seeming intelligence, whom the rebels suspected of being a spy or a Yankee. I was anxious to have a talk with him, but I feared it might excite suspicion against myself, and so refrained. As I had collected enough bread by this time to supply me for several days, and had also completely filled the aching void beneath my jacket, I began considering the situation. I reasoned that I was liable to be sent at any time to the rebel regiment to which I had satisfied the Provost Marshall I belonged, and in that case I should, when my fraudulent representation was discovered, be sent to Castle Thunder. Hence my only hope of avoiding such a calamity was in escaping from the retreat. I had been thinking of this, but the chance seemed almost overwhelming against succeeding, as the place was so thoroughly guarded, and a sentry always accompanied an inmate when he had occasion to visit the outhouse.

I traded my shoes for a pair of rebel shoes, which were tan colored, and I had exchanged my blue cap for a rebel cap and received a dollar to boot, and I had sold the two handkerchiefs that I had stolen from the knapsack of my guard on the train for nine dollars, so I had ten dollars cash capital, beside the several day's rations of bread, so I felt that I was pretty comfortably fixed for almost any kind of an enterprise. Besides, I now had a full-fledged rebel uniform, excepting the pants, and as a great many of their soldiers wore blue pants, which they had taken from prisoners, I was easy on that score.

At this time both Lee's and Early's armies were in desperate need of recruits, and the three hundred North Carolina conscripts, of whom I have spoken, were divided equally between those two armies. Thinking that I saw a glimmer of hope of escape in this allotment of men, I just put myself in position to be counted off with the Tar-heels which were assigned to Early's army. One morning just about daylight we were marched out of the retreat on the streets of Richmond. While the Johnnies were busily engaged in frantic efforts to get some Tar-heels into an alignment, I was keeping an eye to the main chance, and seeing a favorable opportunity I quietly dodged out between two of the guards. I slipped up a cross street and escaped them. After walking for awhile I came upon an Irishman who was engaged in taking down the shutters from the windows of a small store. I stepped in and purchased a loaf of wheat bread of about the size of a large rusk, for which I paid one dollar, and a box of matches for half a dollar. I then asked the way to the Fredericksburg railroad station, and being directed I started for that point. I had hastily decided to try the Fredericksburg route again, and on reaching the railroad I started for that city. Two or three miles out this road passed through the outer line of the Richmond fortifications. Here I discovered the works to be so closely guarded that an attempt to get through the lines would be useless. I was obliged to turn back, so returning to Richmond I boldly walked down Broad Street until I reached the Central Depot, and started out down that line again.

After travelling out for several miles, it being a sunny day, I concluded to skirmish for graybacks, as I had had no opportunity of attending to this highly important operation since leaving Belle Isle. So going into a dense thicket I removed my clothing, and found the enemy in strong force, entrenched along the seams of every garment. Soon the crack, crack, of their plump bodies exploding between my thumb nails, sounded like the pattering fire of a distant skirmish line. I set out to keep count of the number slain, but soon concluded that it would be too great a strain on my mental faculties. When I abandoned the count it had extended way up into the hundreds, but I pressed the fight until every enemy was left cold in death on the field. Then replacing my clothing I resumed my tramp, and soon reached the Chickahominy River and succeeded in crossing that historic stream in safety. Its waters were still as black and turbid as when McClellan encamped his magnificent army along its swampy banks. The railroad bridge which spanned the river at this point was a wooden structure, and I was considering the advisability of firing it in daylight when I noticed an apple tree growing near, which had several apples hanging from its boughs. I picked up some stones and was throwing to knock the fruit from the trees, when my block of matches went off in my pocket, and the means of starting a fire, either to damage rebel property or for my own convenience or comfort vanished like a morning dew. The loss of my matches fell upon me like a crushing calamity, especially when I remembered how I had previously suffered in my efforts to escape, without means of starting a fire by which to cook a morsel of food or to warm my frost benumbed limbs, and I just sat down on the end of a tie and cried, as though some great grief had overtaken me.

In looking back over the conditions which at that time surrounded me I can clearly discern the hand of a kind Providence in the loss of that block of matches, for if I had been possessed of the means of so doing I would have doubtless fired that bridge, and later, I would have fallen into the hands of the enemy, with the charge of wantonly destroying property standing over against me. As the rebels executed without mercy any person against whom an act of vandalism was proven, the jig would have been all up with me. And another thing, which after the lapse of time and much cool reflection, I have never been able to fully comprehend, how could I ever have hoped to escape from the network of obstacles with which I was surrounded, without information in regard to the topography of the country or the position of the enemy's lines, or in fact anything else which a man lacking a faithful guide could have built the slightest hope upon to aid him in escaping. I have, however, concluded that it must have been the recollection of the ease with which I had fooled the provost and traversed the streets of Richmond in broad daylight unquestioned. I say I am quite sure that these master strokes of diplomacy, as I was pleased to regard them, were the procuring cause of this rash undertaking.

One very important thing in regard to circumstances as they existed in Richmond I had failed to take into account. There the people felt secure, because they were, so to speak, within the walls of their city, where they had no thought of a Yankee spy or any other Yankee being at large. But it was different in the suburbs and outside the lines of the fortifications of the city proper. Here the people stood in momentary fear and expectation of cavalry raids and were suspicious of everyone not belonging to their immediate neighborhood. And in regard to my success in imposing upon the Provost Marshall I do not believe there was an intelligent rebel in all Richmond who for one moment supposed that there was any Yankee so devoid of the proverbial astuteness and caution of the race, as to attempt to pass himself off as a rebel soldier and masquerade through the streets of the city in uniform, half Reb and half Yank.

After bemoaning for awhile the loss of my matches, I resumed my journey, sad and to some extent dispirited, and on arriving in sight of the fort at the South Anna River, where I was captured on the occasion of my former attempt to escape, I turned aside into the bushes and lay concealed until the shade of night had fallen over the scene. I then started out again, making a sweeping detour to the right, thus striking the river below the fort. I stripped off my clothing and swam the stream, and a cold bath it was, I can assure you, for the night was chilly and frosty, and on getting out of the water I was seized with a severe rigor, and was scarcely able to dress myself, my teeth rattling like castanets. I feared that this chattering would be heard by the rebels in the fort. With great difficulty I made off and soon coming to a field of shocked corn, I crawled under a shock and remained for a time, in hope of getting my chilled blood to circulate more freely. In time I was disappointed, for the longer I remained the colder I became, and so was obliged to resume my tramp.

About daylight I came upon a small hut occupied by a negro family. It was surrounded by woods, near the railroad, and there was standing in the door of the cabin a middle-aged negress, who upon my approach stepped out and asked me if I had any clothing of which I wished to dispose. I replied in the negative and passed on. In this I realized later on that I had made a mistake, for here was an opportunity of disposing of my blue vest and blouse, the silent witnesses of my being a Yankee soldier. I should have taken immediate advantage of this chance, and without doubt I could have made myself known with perfect safety and probably been assisted through the lines, or at the least have obtained valuable information in regard to the country through which I must pass if I escaped at all, but being fearful of betrayal I passed on to my fate.

It was still early morning when I arrived at Hanover Junction. Our cavalry having recently burned the bridge at that point, all passengers had to be transferred there. The Fredericksburg train was standing there awaiting the arrival of the Richmond train, and as I walked by the engine the engineer eyed me very closely, but said nothing, and I trudged on in the direction of Fredericksburg. Several miles out of Hanover, as I was passing through a sand cut on the railroad, I encountered a blowing adder, and it seemed to dispute my passage, as it was coiled ready for a spring. It kept up a hissing which would have done credit to a full grown "gray gander." He was a large fellow, and as there was neither club nor stone to be found in the cut, I skirmished around and finally secured a piece of rotten tie, which showed its weakness at every blow. But by dint of perseverance I finally managed to kill the reptile. I was much surprised to find a snake abroad at that season of the year, it being well into the month of October, but he evidently was out for business, as he made no effort to escape while I was searching for something with which to slay him.

Shortly after getting through the cut, the train which I had passed while it was standing at the junction, passed me on its way to Fredericksburg, and again that engineer eyed me very suspiciously. About noon, as I sat resting, concealed in some bushes, two men with guns and dogs made their appearance on the opposite side of the railroad, and it looked for a time as though I should be discovered. They finally went on their way, and I again resumed my line of march. Toward evening I arrived at Guinea Station, eight miles distant from Fredericksburg. This place was made up of a water tank on one side of the railroad and three or four houses on the other side, one of which stood near the track.

As I passed the house of which I spoke as standing near the track, a woman who was sitting in the door with her sewing, asked me for the news of the day and I paused long enough to tell her about Mosby's capture of the Yankees in the valley, and started on, laying to my soul the unction that I was safely past another bad place in the road. But as soon as my back was turned a rebel soldier came out of the house, and stealing softly up behind me ordered me to halt, and on facing about, I found myself gazing into the muzzle of a big navy revolver. His questions came thick and fast. "Who are you?" "Where do you belong?" And, "Where are you going?" He did not give me time to answer those questions in the prescribed Yankee fashion either, by asking me question for question. But I want to remark that a revolver loaded to the muzzle and in the hands of an enemy, and pointing at you, is a powerful persuader, and had a tendency to sort of make you answer questions whether you want to or not. So, I said my name was Frank Hardy, that I belonged to Mosby's command, that my horse had been killed at Salem in the valley, that I lived near Fredericksburg, and that I was going home to get another horse. I manufactured a lot of other stuff on the spot, all justified I thought, by the ends I sought to accomplish.

The young soldier was favorably impressed by my seemingly straightforward tale and was inclined to let me go, but by this time two or three of the shaggy, tobacco-squirting natives had gathered about us and they strenuously objected to my being released. They said I might be a spy, or an escaped Yankee prisoner, who might bring the Yankee cavalry in to "cut hell outen we'uns." Well, the soldier said he would have nothing more to do with me, so the natives took me in charge, and handed me over to the loving care of a train detective on the arrival of the train from Fredericksburg. This detective was a stalwart six-footer of a fire-eating "Don Furioso," bombastic sort of man. In fact, his hide seemed so stuffed with bombast and self-sufficiency, that one observing him would conclude that if the destinies of the entire Confederacy did not rest wholly upon his shoulders, that he at least was the chief cornerstone.

He took me into the forward car, where there were sitting three or four brutal appearing fellows. Sallow of complexion, they were with countenances which were as pleasant to look upon as that of a Bengal tiger. Stripping off my clothing he examined my pockets, linings and seams, also my cap, its rim, my shoes and shoe soles, and was rewarded for his trouble by finding nothing, as I was not so much of a fool as to commit anything to paper. In answer to his questions I told him that I was unable to read or write. I also gave him the Mosby fabrication, but during his search of my clothing he unearthed from my vest pocket a printed song which he transferred to his pocket. This particular song was entitled, "The Arms of Abraham." The first verse and chorus were as follows, and will, I think, be recognized by all comrades:

"My true love is a soldier in the army now today,
T'was this cruel war that made him, he had to go away.
The draft it was that took him, it was a cruel blow,

It took him for a conscript, but he didn't want to go."

Chorus:

"He's gone, he's gone, as meek as any lamb.
They took him, yes, they took him, to the arms of Abraham."

As soon as I had replaced my garments, the detective turned suddenly and handing me the song said, "Sing that song for us!" "Oh, I can't read," said I, handing it back to him. He was very angry because of his failure to entrap me, and he exclaimed, "You're a God damn liar!" "I never in my life saw a Yankee who couldn't read and write." As I was not in a position to resent this imputation against my veracity, as the boys say, I was obliged to swallow it. This I did with very good grace, for the compliment paid the Yankee intelligence, in his declaration that they could all read and write, had softened the impeachment greatly. I had begun to lay to my heart the unction that I had successfully baffled him, when he reached for my bundle, and untying it he brought out my blue vest and blouse. He was not furious, and drawing his revolver and placing it within a foot of my forehead said, "You son-of-a-bitch of a Yankee, I've a mind to blow yo' brains out, and by God I would shoot yo', but I'll have yo' hung for a spy when I gen yo' to Richmond." Under these embarrassing circumstances I could say nothing, but I looked him in the eye until he lowered his revolver, then I calmly sat down on a seat next to the window and observed the landscape as we whirled by it.

I hoped to discover some scene of beauty which might serve to divert my mind from its unpleasant occupation. Those tiger-faced men, to whom reference has been made, sat there taking no part in the conversation, but evidently enjoying the act much as a theater-goer might the tragedy just at the point where the villain is to be detected and exposed. On arriving at Hanover Junction, where the train halted for a short time, I purchased some apples from a lad at the car window, at which I nonchalantly munched all the way into Richmond, and while outwardly I appeared so careless and composed, there was a tumult transpiring within. Indeed, I was fearfully agitated and distressed, for I was now about to be brought face to face with the same Provost

Marshall as a spy, upon whom a few days previous I had imposed myself as a rebel soldier. I could but think, "Ah, now there's the rub." However, I had braced myself for the interview, and by the time we arrived at the office, I had determined to give my correct name and a full account of my first escape only, as I thought this would tally with the register at Libby, and have a tendency to divert suspicion from me as a spy in case they should accuse me of that offense. I must admit that the bearing of my captor, upon arriving at Richmond, was anything but reassuring, as my "Furioso" marched me through the streets, swinging his big revolver like a conquering hero, his air of importance, and the majesty of his swagger seeming to indicate that he felt his importance to be great. He seemed to expect the populace to turn out en masse to greet him with "Hail to the Chief," or, "See the Conquering Hero Comes." But they did not, and on reaching the provost's presence, I observed that "Furioso's" airs suddenly collapsed and I gathered from the marshall's manner toward him, that he knew him as a chronic blowhard and a brainless bully. The marshall asked him where I had been taken, and if I had been carefully searched, and if so, if any incriminating evidence in the way of papers or any documents had been discovered, and then very curtly dismissed him.

I was then ordered up, and in reply to the questions of the provost I answered, giving my name, company and regiment, all the time keeping my face as much in the shade as possible. I stated that I had escaped from the car on the way to Salisbury, and had been recaptured, and to my great comfort and delight, neither the marshall nor his clerk recognized me as the Frank Hardy who had passed as a rebel soldier and been sent to the soldier's retreat. Making out a commitment, he called a guard who conducted me, in company with another prisoner, down to Castle Thunder. This disheartened me greatly, as I was aware that only such as were to be arraigned for some offense against the Confederacy were confined there.

Castle Thunder, to the Yankees confined within its gloomy walls, was a veritable dungeon of despair. All hope of exchange or parole died, and he was released only after trial, if convicted, to be executed, and to be sent back to Libby if exonerated. Dante's description over the portals of Hades would have been appropriate above the gates of Castle

Thunder: "Abandon hope, all ye who enter here." A mighty burden was rolled off my soul when upon reaching the prison only the other man, the prisoner who accompanied me from the provost's office, was left at that inferno.

Chapter Twelve

IMPRISONED AGAIN IN LIBBY

I was taken across the street to Dick Turner's office and then confined on the ground floor in the west end of the building. I soon found that my fellow prisoners on that floor were all negro soldiers. I being the only white man in the room and dressed as I was in a rebel uniform, I was at first suspected by them of being a rebel spy. I succeeded in convincing them, however, that I was a Yankee in disguise and then questioned them as to where they had been captured and learned what I could in regard to what had been transpiring outside since I had been a prisoner. These poor fellows seemed to me to be overworked, and I asked them what they had been doing. They informed me that they had fallen into the rebel's hands at Fort Harrison, and that since their arrival at Libby they had been marched out every day and made to work in constructing rebel fortifications, one of the most flagrant breeches of the usages of modern warfare. Yet I blush to say that our government made no protest against this great wrong, and, so far as I was ever able to learn, made no effort to prevent it, or to protect these colored soldiers in their rights as prisoners of war. I could not have believed it possible that such treatment would have been imposed upon prisoners of war, and the government to whom they belonged, made no protestation against it. But I saw morning after morning, these soldiers marched out and put to work on the rebel works, where they toiled all day, to be marched back in the evening, so I know there can be no possible doubt in regard to the matter.

General B. F. Butler, who about this time was engaged in digging the war exigency device, the Dutch Gap Canal, heard of what the rebels were doing to our negro soldiers, and that brave and humane man on his own responsibility notified General Robert E. Lee that if the practice was not immediately stopped he would at once put an equal number of rebel officers to work on the Dutch Gap Canal. General Lee answered, denying positively that any United States soldiers were being worked on their fortifications. General Butler, whose information must have been of a reliable nature, refused to accept Lee's denial, and accordingly put the rebel officers to work on the canal. This procedure put a sudden stop to the working of the negro troops on rebel fortifications. In the meantime, I obtained a copy of the "Richmond Dispatch," which contained the correspondence which passed between Butler and Lee on the subject. As a consequence, I watched the result closely and observed that the colored soldiers were not marched out in the morning. I questioned the men after they had been withdrawn from their labor on the works, therefore I know that this statement is absolutely true. And yet the highest officer in the rebel army, General Robert E. Lee, the supposed soul of southern honor, knowingly and deliberately lied, in the interests of a traitorous rebellion. All honor, I say, to the name of Ben Butler, who at least to the extent of his ability and authority, undertook to protect the poor prisoners of war who it seems to me the government wantonly abandoned to death by starvation. They never put forth more than feeble and unavailing efforts to protect and defend the prisoners from the cruel indignities heaped upon them by their brutal captors. Hurrah for Old Spoony! He always served an effectual remedy in heroic doses for the cure of treason, and that fact the rebels duly appreciated, as was attested by them in the fact that they kept a standing reward of one hundred thousand dollars in gold on his head, "dead or alive."

On the two floors above the negro quarters, in Libby, white men were confined and as the prison keepers always took down the communicating stair at night, I slept the first night among the negroes. The next morning I chanced to get under the hatchway or opening loft for the stairs and I heard someone shout, "By God, if here ain't old Father Darby!" "Father" was the nickname by which I was called in my company. Upon looking up I beheld the smiling face of David Ritchie, and others of my company. Coming to the opening they let down a blanket which I laid hold of and they soon landed me on a higher plane. On this floor I found as partners in distress the following comrades: Isaac N. Mitchell, of Uniontown; Leslie Francis, of Perryopolis; David Ritchie, of New Haven; Calvin Darnell, of Grindstone; and Bartholemew Warman, of Dunbar. All of these men had escaped through the hole I had kicked in the end of the car, but like myself had been retaken and returned to Libby several days before I was sent back to keep them company. After a hearty greeting, we related to each other our experiences and while they were somewhat varied, they all had the same sad sequence, in that we each and all failed to make good our escape to "God's Country," as the North was called by the boys.

Darnell and Warman had gotten fifty miles away before being captured. They were sighted by a planter who had a gang of slaves engaged in cutting a field of tobacco. He started them in pursuit of the two soldiers, armed with their tobacco knives. Warman was taken, but when Darnell's pursuer got close enough, Darnell, without stopping, turned his head and shouted, "Slack up! Slack up, Dammit, what do you want to take me for?" The negro then pretended to be winded, slackened his pace, and allowed Darnell to run away from him. He made his way to the rebel General Malone's line in Petersburg, and was concealed by a negro for two days at Malone's headquarters. He was, however, retaken on attempting to run the lines. Mitchell, Ritchie and Francis had made their way one hundred miles from Richmond and then had been run down by bloodhounds and recaptured. Darnell had been given a silver dollar by a slave. It was the only money the poor fellow had. With this dollar he had bought the blanket with which they hoisted me to the second floor on the morning after my arrival at Libby.

On this floor Francis had been placed in command. It was his duty to form the men in double line for the monster, Dick Turner, to count off each morning, and also to report the sick. For this service he received on extra ration of bread each day. There were eighty-three of us in this room at the time, and among them were the men who saw me pass myself off as a rebel soldier on the captain in the car as they were being taken to Richmond. These fellows told the other prisoners of the episode in the car, and it created a strong prejudice against me, as they thought me a rebel spy. They probably would have made it very uncomfortable for me had it not been for the assurance given them by my comrades that I was alright. After I explained to them how this all came about, I was immediately taken into full communion and good fellowship.

The nights now were quite cool and we had no fire. There was neither glass nor sash in the windows, and in order to keep warm we slept spoon fashion along the walls. We lay so close that when one fellow wanted to whop over the whole line had to whop. Frequently during the night some poor starving skeleton, whose sharp hip bones were cutting through to the hard floor, cried out, "Turn over up there!" If anyone neglected or refused to obey the injunction to turn the air would be full of impeachments against the tardy one.

Amongst the prisoners was a young cavalryman, from Wisconsin, I believe. He was the fortunate owner of a blanket which he kindly offered to share with me. As my five comrades were already taxing the ductile qualities of their one blanket to its utmost, I gratefully accepted this kindness. After sharing the hospitality of my new found friend for several consecutive nights, I was greatly pained and astonished by being accused by him of having robbed him during the night. I was very indignant at the accusation and felt the hot blood of shame and anger rushing to my cheeks. I could hardly refrain from assaulting him on the spot, but finally I cooled off sufficiently to inquire of him as to whether he had been stirring about any during the night. Indeed, I had been awakened by his getting up in the night. He answered that he had been to the sink. I told him to go there and find his money, or I should be obliged to wipe up the floors of Libby with his dirty lying body. While he was gone I pulled off my jacket and cleared the deck for action, for really I had no thought of his finding his money where there were so many chances of its having been picked up. It had fallen from his watch-fob pocket, and there it lay just as it had fallen. To accuse a comrade of stealing it! I gave him a lecture, couched in language which at this distant day is remembered by me as being more emphatic than elegant. I told my messmates what had occurred and they were angry and wanted to thrash him. I finally prevailed on them to allow the matter to drop, which it did. But I foreswore that chap as a bedfellow ever after that.

Francis was taken sick and was sent to the prison hospital, and I was promoted to the position made vacant by his disability and I then had the right by dint of my promotion to sleep under the protecting folds of one-fifth of the blanket which had sheltered him during his tenure of office as commander of that room. At the window, near the stairway, there was a loose brick in the wall, and one of the men took it one night to use as a pillow. On the following morning at the designated hour, I had the alignment made, ready for counting off. Dick Turner, on coming up the stairs, saw that a brick had been displaced from the wall, whereupon he instantly fell into a towering rage. He began raving and cursing all Yankees in general, and the one who took that brick in particular. He swore. "Not a God damned Yankee in this room will have anything to eat or drink until the son-of-a-bitch is found who took that brick!" He then stationed guards at either end of the line with orders to shoot "the first damned Yankee" who dared to move out of his tracks. Leaving us in this desperate position, he went to the floor above. Now, while the loss of one daily meal to a hearty, well man, would hardly be regarded as a hardship, to men near starvation, the loss of the same meant real suffering. The torture of standing in line, not daring to change position under pain of death, further weakened the boys, many of whom were already in an emaciated physical condition. The older prisoners, well knowing the devilish, cruel character of Dick Turner, advised the man who had taken the brick that he should confess, and thus save the innocent more needless suffering. This was done. The man had been a prisoner for only a few days and was completely innocent of any malicious intent. On the return of Turner to the room, I explained the facts to him and pleaded the inexperience of the offender. I told him the brick had been only lying against the wall just where the man had left it on getting up from his rest on the floor in the morning. Without making any reply to me he whipped out a large revolver and pointing it at the man, with a horrible oath, exclaimed, "Put that brick back where you got it from, and if you ever touch another brick in this wall I'll blow your brains out, God damn you!" He then counted us off, and relieved us of his damnable presence for that occasion.

It seems to me quite proper at this juncture to pause sufficiently long to pay to this "duet of hell," a passing compliment. Turner, the unmatched villain and miscreant, showed his cowardly, disreputable and brutal character in the trivial incidents of the brick and cartridge, better than I could hope to paint in words. In fact, the English language fails to furnish words of the requisite shades of blackness to properly characterize the infamy of the heart of this miserable man. If God ever created this travesty of man in his own likeness, some malevolent power succeeded in completely perverting the work, for he certainly embodied in his vile character all the characteristics of the Prince of

Devils. He was strong, stocky of build, of medium height, swarthy complexion, with thick, curly hair. I am sure the declaration of scripture, that "out of the abundance of the heart the mouth speaketh," found verification in him for he was possessed of a vocabulary rich in profanity and vile that would have caused the proverbial fishwife to hide her head in shame. I think that the oft repeated declaration that no bullying, boasting, brutal braggart, ever made a good soldier is essentially true, and that fact probably explains why Dick Turner held the position of overseer of Libby Prison. He was simply too great a coward to enter the rebel army and fight like a man against men for a principle which he professed to hold dear. He preferred to have the enemy against whom he was to fight, cooped up and disarmed so that his dastardly carcass would be in no danger or harm. Dick Turner stole the pennies from the eyes of a dead friend, and then seriously mutilated the corpse. As often as once a week he would fall into a particularly cheerful frame of mind and upon such occasions he told us that torpedoes were arranged under the prison to blow us all to pieces if the Yankee cavalry came to rescue us. In spite of this often repeated piece of information, the prisoners to a man wished and longed for the arrival of our cavalry. Pity, generosity or compassion were wholly unknown to him and in his intercourse with the Yankees he was totally devoid of the finer sensibilities of humanity.

Dick Turner's accomplice was one Lieutenant Boissieux. Nearly all the indictments against the former will serve for the latter. This detestable, cowardly, low-lived villain, also no doubt held his position at Belle Isle for the same reasons and on account of the same qualifications that Turner did at Libby.

He was French by birth, was of a slight build, much more slender in person than Turner, but he evidently developed about as much depravity to the square inch as did that hellion. I have already told of the punishment through the agency of the wooden horse which Boissieux inflicted on the men who endeavored to escape by swimming to the little isle. The severity and awful suffering this brought its victims showed the innate brutality of the man. I watched this wretch snatch a musket from the hands of a guard and spring like a panther into the midst of a crowd of prisoners, and without cause or provocation, with the butt of the gun, indiscriminately knock to the right and left the weak, starved creatures before him. He also made a standing proposition to the rebel prison guard that whoever killed a Yankee prisoner could have a thirty day furlough. Several men were murdered because of this. Our government never uttered one word of protest. I am aware, however, of some apologists who have undertaken to explain this away by urging that it was because the rebels refused to extend the right of parole or exchange to the negro troops who had fallen into their hands.

There were a couple of incidents which occurred on the island before my arrival there as a prisoner which I will relate as they were told to me by an eyewitness. Boissieux had a pet black and tan terrier which one day strayed into camp. A prisoner caught it, cut its throat, skinned and prepared to cook it. Boissieux, missing his pet, suspected it had gotten into camp. He hurried in and observed a man in the act of building a fire with a bit of wood. The lieutenant approached and discovered his dog ready for roasting. He was furious and drawing his revolver, exclaimed, "Now, you God damn son-of-a-bitch, eat that dog and eat him raw, or I'll blow your brains out!" The man who was so near starved that he could hardly wait to cook it anyhow, went at it and soon had its bones polished, while Boissieux, who waited to see the last morsel disappear, withdrew. The man waited until he was out of hearing, shook his fist at him, and said, "Oh, you rebel son-of-a-bitch, you thought you were punishing me, didn't you?" Then wiping his mouth on his sleeve said, "I only wish I had another dog to eat."

One day a guard whose beat ran from the river to the camp on the outside of the fence along the lane, shot and killed a prisoner as he was returning with a bucket of water from the river. A Buck Tail, who had seen the killing, armed himself with a shin bone and slipped down along the fence. He reached over and struck the guard a fearful blow on the head, which killed him. Boissieux shut off the rations of the camp and swore he would starve every "damned Yankee" to death unless the man who killed the guard was found. The men became desperate and threatening by evening and Boissieux's cowardly heart failed him. Fearing a prison revolt he rushed the grub into camp.

Being in the western end of the Libby prison, we commanded a good view of the wharf, where we used to stand behind the bars to watch the rebels land from the exchange boats. Fat, hearty, saucy and happy, they would run down the gangplank onto the wharf shouting and hurrahing for Jeff Davis and the Southern Confederacy. They'd kick up their heels like a lot of colts on being turned into a field of fresh clover. After a little, a miserable, melancholy procession of Yankees from the hospitals, to be exchanged for those hearty, well-fed rebels, would appear slowly and painfully stagger toward the boat. A great number of them would be unable to walk at all, and had to be carried aboard the boat on stretchers. Now I am reminded of another reason assigned by our government for stopping the exchange of prisoners, one which I was taunted regularly with by the rebels. The rebels, on being released from our northern prisons, were ready to enter immediately into their armies of service, while the Yankees, if they survived at all, were so reduced by starvation that it would be months before they were ready for field service. The proper way to have corrected this evil would have been to have furnished the rebel prisoners with the same kind and quality of food, shelter and clothing that was furnished us by them. Not following this course of action placed the Union prisoner of war at a great disadvantage and was unjust. The golden rule of warfare should be, "Whatsoever the enemy doeth unto you, do ye also unto the enemy." If one of the belligerents wages a war of brutal savagery, the more humane party will be the sufferer every time unless he responds in kind. Seventy-one thousand men died as a result of the cruel savagery practiced upon them by the rebels, in whose hands they were kept as prisoners of war while no corresponding loss was inflicted upon Confederate prisoners by the Federal government. I hold it to be true that it would have been quite as humane to have starved to death rebels who were in armed rebellion, as to starve to death Union men who were striving to maintain the government and preserve their national life. Any country engaged in a war, and refusing or neglecting to protect its soldiery by an equitable system of reprisal and retaliation, is unworthy of its support.

The view obtained from the windows of Libby were necessarily distant ones, as we were forbidden on penalty of being instantly shot down, from approaching nearer than several feet to the sills of the windows. The guards would shoot anyone going near enough to the bars to be seen by them from the street below. One of our rooms was ornamented with a stove of the common variety, but the rebels would allow us no fire. There were several boxes of sawdust in the room which were used as spittoons, and were as a rule in a very filthy condition, yet I have seen starving men pick bones out of this mass of filth and corruption and gnaw at them most ravenously.

About the 1st of November, 1864, Dick Turner accompanied by several other rebels came into the prison room and selected me for the position of hospital wardmaster to serve in a hospital which they were about to establish for the care (or, perhaps more properly, the slow death), of a number of sick and wounded Yankees who had been taken in one of our hospitals at or near Fort Harrison. They accorded to me as wardmaster the privilege of selecting four men to act as nurses, and one to serve as hospital steward, from among my fellow prisoners. I selected Mitchell, Darnell, Ritchie and Warman for nurses, and a man by the name of Fogle for steward. Fogle was one of the men taken by Mosby, and was on the train at the time I passed myself off on the captain as a rebel soldier. Fogle assured me that he was well posted upon the subject of medicines, having, as he said, served as a prescription clerk in a drug store. However, when he undertook to fill prescriptions I found him to be an unmitigated liar, as he knew absolutely nothing about medicines, not so much as a mule might be expected to know of mathematics. I did not particularly blame him, however, as he took this course to get out of a living hell. On the contrary, I assisted him all I could, and as our "materia medica" was not elaborate, it required no proficient Latin to handle it successfully. We got along fairly well after that. If Fogle is still in the land of the living I should be pleased to take a pill with him for the sake of "Auld Lang Syne."

We were inducted into our newly found field of usefulness in a large three-story brick tobacco house which fronted on Broad Street; the building and grounds were enclosed with a high board fence. There was a two-story frame addition to the brick building which also fronted on Broad Street, the upper story of which was used as a sleeping room in common by the attendants of the three wards composing the hospital.

The lower floor of this building was partially filled with stems and refuse tobacco, covering the floor to the depth of several feet. To this room we had free access. Now directly across from the main or brick portion of the building was a small brick structure which was used as a gangrene ward.

My comrades and I were assigned to duty on the upper floor which was furnished with cots for about fifty patients. We drew soup, which was very thin, its chief ingredients being rice and potatoes, skins and all, but as our patients did not arrive until long after the dinner hour, Mr. Woodward, the steward in charge, allowed us to eat as much of the soup as we desired. I am here to say that my five assistants and I got away with it slick and clean, thus taking a fairly good fill up on the ration which would have had to answer for the fifty men had they arrived in time for dinner. Darnell, although a small man, managed to eat an ordinary wooden bucket full of the soup, which so distended his proportions that it was impossible for him to flex his body, and in consequence he was obliged to sit upright as stiff as a ramrod.

This hospital was really but an annex to General Hospital Number 21, from which our food and medicine were obtained and to which our dead were carried. This general hospital, if my memory serves me correctly, was located at the corner of Cary and a cross street, one square distant from ours, and when any of us had occasion to go there, we were attended by rebel guards. In emergency cases, where a doctor of remedies was needed promptly, this awaiting the motion of the guard caused a delay which in numerous instances proved fatal to the patient, whereas prompt action would have saved the life of the sufferer.

Towards evening of our initial day at the hospital annex, our expected patients arrived and were promptly installed upon their respective cots, many, alas, of whom were never to leave them in life. I had but one case of amputation in my department, and that was performed upon a cavalryman by the name of O'Brian. He was a member of a New York regiment, the number of which has escaped me. The leg was amputated below the knee. I had numerous cases of gunshot wounds, some of which were very severe. The other patients were sufferers mainly from desperate attacks of pneumonia, chronic diarrhoea, scurvy, diphtheria, pleurisy, typhoid and remittent fevers. Our ward was fumigated daily by a negro attendant who walked silently up one aisle and down another bearing in his hands a shovel of coals upon which was burning coal tar or pitch. This operation was performed in the mornings before the arrival of the doctor on his daily rounds. Our "materia medica" embraced the following named, well recognized drugs and remedies: aqua-pura; sheep's tallow for dressing amputations; Spanish fly and mustard for blisters or counter irritants; flaxseed for poultices; nitrate of silver as a caustic; opium and corn whisky as stimulants; tincture and iodine of iron, and perhaps a few other drugs of like character. We had no quinine or chincona, or anything of that kind.

Chapter Thirteen

WOODWARD

I beg leave to introduce you to Mr. Woodward. He was a resident of Richmond, Virginia, a merchant by avocation, whom I strongly suspect of occupying his position of hospital superintendent only to avoid service in the rebel army. Mr. Woodward was a genial, pleasant, mild-mannered man, a little above medium height; good humor seemed to be his ruling characteristic. He was so striking an exception to the average rebel official that I cannot pass him by without a kindly word. In all the time of my association with him I never knew him to be guilty of applying an abusive or profane epithet to a Yankee, nor did I ever see him display an angry mood. His good humor bubbled up from the midst of his vile environments and sparkled forth like an oasis, in a Sahara of disgusting obscenity, vituperation and profane abuse. His business requiring most of his time, his visits to the institution resembled the proverbial angel visits; they were few and far between, usually no more than once or twice a week. He, however, had an assistant in the person of one Charles Walters, who occupied a room on the second floor of the annex, where a space had been partitioned off for that purpose.

Mr. Woodward was in general good favor with the prisoners, and well liked by them. At heart he was really a Union man, a fact he more than intimated to me upon several occasions. He told me that it was the universal belief in Richmond, at that time, that if General George B. McClellan were to be elected President, that the Confederacy would become an instant success. This view was also held by Charles Walters, who was a rebel in every respect, as well as a number of rebel officers at Belle Isle and Libby. Many southerners believed that if McClellan defeated Lincoln in the national election of 1864, the south would finally be victorious. In searching for the causes of the rebel faith in McClellan's desire and ability to save them, it will be necessary to review the Peninsular and Antietam campaigns, or at least such portions of them as may testify to his incompetent and treasonable acts. The rebels developed such a liking for McClellan that they repeatedly cheered for him from behind their breastworks. Many comrades could testify to this.

McClellan collected immense numbers of small arms and large quantities of munitions, but failed to issue them to his own troops, notwithstanding that thousands of his soldiers were armed with useless Harper's Ferry muskets. The fact of his leaving thousands of stands of those new Springfield rifles, together with numberless munitions which he allowed to fall into the hands of the enemy, rendered him dear to the rebel heart. Of the millions of dollars worth of military stores collected at White House Landing and Savage Station, only a small fraction were ever destroyed, the balance of which was purposely left for the rebel army. This explains why the Johnnies referred to him as being the best quartermaster they ever had.

The Fifth Army Corps occupied the north side of the Chickahominy, and the balance of the army was on the south or Richmond side of the river, with three bridges connecting them; one at Deep Bottom, the railroad bridge at Dispatch Station, and one still lower down the stream. General Lee, leaving Magruder in the defense of Richmond with twenty-five thousand troops, crossed the Chickahominy at Hanover Junction twenty-three miles from Richmond, and being reinforced by Jackson, attacked the right of the Fifth Corps at Mechanicsville. The Union line at this point was held by the division of the Pennsylvania Reserves under General McCall and the Reserves fought the battle on that part of the line without assistance from the rest of the corps. The rebels were badly defeated and suffered a severe loss in killed and wounded, while our losses were minimal. The next day, at Gaines' Mill, the losses were about evenly divided. At Mechanicsville, the Confederate loss was six thousand, so in the two battles, the overall results were in favor of the Union Army.

The Fifth Corps was then withdrawn to the Richmond side of the river and the bridges were destroyed. It seemed opportune to hurl the victorious Army of the Potomac down upon Magruder at Richmond. Magruder was separated at that point from both Jackson and Lee. General Fremont's army was free to go to the defense of Washington. Lee would have been obliged to rebuild the bridges over the

Chickahominy or to have taken a circular route via Hanover Junction, delaying him from Richmond by thirty-six to forty-eight crucial hours. In that time the Army of the Potomac could have engulfed Richmond and defeated its defenders. But it was not to be.

General McClellan knew the bravery of his men, and the devotion of his army. On the contrary, he feared the intensity of their courage and patriotism. He guarded against the army inflicting irreparable injury upon the enemy, with whom he was in undoubted sympathy. His unexplained and inexcusable delays are easily accounted for when we consider that time, with the rebels, was the great desideratum. It was time they needed, time to fortify, time to recruit and replenish, in fact, time was their only hope of salvation. Richmond, at that point, was in a state of complete panic, and Little Mac, ever the unready, lavishly granted them time galore. General Heintzelman said after the Battle of Fair Oaks, "I have no doubt but that we might have gone right into Richmond." Heintzelman's opinion was shared by almost every officer in that army whose knowledge of the situation entitled them to consideration. And if this could have been done after the Battle of Fair Oaks, against the whole rebel army, how much more easily it could have been accomplished after the Battle of Gaines' Mill, when only Magruder and his twenty-five thousand men were in defense.

The losses of the two armies in killed and wounded in the series of battles which culminated in the Battle of Malvern Hill, were about equal, if we except Mechanicsville and Malvern, where the rebel losses far exceeded those of the Union Army. It is a matter of history that at Malvern Hill General McClellan abandoned his army and took refuge on a gunboat six miles distant from the field. He was not on the ground anytime during the progress of the fight. In fact, during all of my term of service in the Army of the Potomac, I never saw him under fire in any battle. Surely these were not the actions of a brave, loyal general who was true to his country and desired to see its army victorious in the field. McClellan always made sure of his own safety, even while the brave boys under his command were in the most perilous danger.

At the opening of the Battle of Malvern Hill the Corps Commanders formed in line in an open field without defenses or protection of any kind. The combined forces of Lee and Jackson were augmented by Magruder and their lines were well protected by dense woods. We had lost about fifteen thousand men up to this point and were now outnumbered by about ten thousand of the enemy. Despite the hardships of the last seven days of battle, the Army of the Potomac met the enemy at Malvern Hill and defeated them at every point. We accomplished this even though our commanding officer was skulking aboard a gunboat. Oh, for a Phil Sheridan at this supreme moment! There would have been a total rout of the rebels and the spoils of victory would have been ours. The utter destruction of the Confederate Army was again possible. McClellan, however, ordered a retreat, thus allowing the chaplet of victory, so heroically earned by his gallant army, to be borne off by their defeated foemen. General Philip Kearny stated, "I, Philip Kearny, an old soldier, do most solemnly enter my protest against this order for a retreat. We ought instead of retreating to follow up the enemy and take Richmond, and in full view of all the responsibilities of such a declaration I say to you all, such an order can only be prompted by cowardice or treason!" These strong words coming from a general against his commanding officer are further evidence testifying to the incompetence of McClellan in the field.

At Antietam, a flag of truce suspending hostilities for a space of twenty-four hours was granted Lee by McClellan, while a decisive battle was rapidly being decided in favor of the Union cause. Such a procedure in the whole course of the war up to that time had never been thought of, neither was such an action taken by a commander of either army during the remainder of the war. I feel safe in saying that history fails to furnish a parallel to this. The truce saved Lee's army from total annihilation. Lee escaped to the Virginia shore. Every dead soldier on the battlefield of Antietam was a sacrificial offering to the Moloch of rebellion, while the responsible general went free of all punishment.

I now return to the hybrid individual who was second in command at the hospital. This person, of course, was Charles Walters. He was a rouged, painted, effeminate, weakly, dried up individual with an angular face almost sharp enough to shoot fish with. This apology of a man was most heartily detested by the Yankees and was always spoken of by them as belonging to the female sex. He was supposed to be, and no doubt was, a played-out member of the Richmond demi monde, dressed in male attire. Walters always made his appearance in the morning freshly rouged and painted with a dudish and dandified air ill befitting his threadbare and overworn garments. Walter's sharp cheek bones protruded from a withered and painted face like bumps on a peeled log. This man would select a young and good looking Yankee for a patient and pet, much as an old maid would be expected to select a kitten or poodle. I often saw Walters having a jolly time lavishing maudlin affections upon his young favorite in his room.

When Woodward, the superintendent, paid his visits, "Charlie" always had a long string of complaints and charges to pour into his ears about the terrible Yankees. Woodward, on such occasions, would chuck Walters under the chin and laugh and joke to make light of the latter's angry mood. He never took action on any of these complaints and considered them to be the mere vaporings of an antique and ill-humored old maid. When Walters railed against Ritchie and Warman, the men threatened to throw him out of a window. They were confined for this in a room called the "retaliation room."

Chapter Fourteen

DISCIPLES OF AESCULAPIUS

Our hospitals afforded to the fledglings of Aesculapius and the nonentities styling themselves as physicians, an elegant opportunity, which by the way they were not slow to avail themselves of, to practice their art, or rather to demonstrate their ignorance of the principles of the science which they affected to be masters of. As the prisoners had no friends to protest against their being subjects for the experiments of harlequins and their unskilled and senseless treatment, the consequence was that changes in "surgeons" were frequent.

Among the patients in my department was a vigorous, hearty German who had been hit high up on the forehead by a bullet, causing a depression of the skull at that point, resulting in compression of the brain and causing the most excruciating pain. Obviously, relieving the pressure was the thing needed, which could have been readily accomplished by trepanning, and such a course would doubtless have saved the life of the sufferer. One morning a bleary-eyed, stupid looking individual, announcing himself as a doctor came in, and after walking through the aisles of the ward, prescribed either a flaxseed poultice or a mustard plaster for every patient in the place, excepting only the man who had suffered an amputation of the leg. A poultice was accordingly applied to the poor German's head. The result of this process was to further tax the weakened brain with blood. In response to this irritant, and as a direct consequence, the patient died the following morning. I mention this case in order to show the reader the danger to life and limb the soldier is subject, even though he might succeed in escaping death on the battlefield. And it is a fact beyond controversy that there were exhibits of fortitude and bravery in the hospitals which equaled, if they did not excel, any displayed on the field of battle.

I must be excused for mentioning a case of extraordinary nerve displayed by a man in my department upon the occasion of the poultice doctor's visit. The name of this hero was Albert Morse. He was a native of the state of Massachusetts and a sailor on the gunboat "Underwriter." He had received a gunshot wound in the shin. He was captured by the rebels at Plymouth and confined for sometime at Charleston, South Carolina. His would had proven very obstinate and the government having abrogated all exchange of prisoners, Morse was sent with many others to Richmond. When the doctor proposed poulticing his wound, he was given to understand in language more expressive than eloquent that the patient would submit to no such nonsense. Reduced in flesh to a virtual skeleton, with a wounded leg in desperate shape, Morse was in a severely weakened condition. The bone for the space of five inches in length was bare of flesh, and to add to this great discomfort, he had three frightful bedsores, one on each hip and one on the back, both of which were at least six inches in diameter. Yet notwithstanding his sufferings, this man exhibited the most determined resolution and courage. Indeed, it would seem impossible, under such surroundings, and in the midst of such suffering, for any human being to have endured with such pluck and nerve. Morse was in no way wary of his language when making known to the doctors his disapproval of their methods. He would roundly curse and damn them daily for refusing to amputate his leg. Gangrene finally set in and he was transferred to the gangrene ward and there submitted to the painful operation of having the affected flesh burned out with nitrate of silver. On being returned to my ward he said to the rebel doctor, "God damn you, why don't you cut that leg off. You think I'll die! But I'll show you that I'll never die in your damned old southern conthieveracy. I'm going to live to get home." The doctors still refused to take the limb off, and in spite of all our efforts to prevent it, gangrene set in again.

The doctors then concluded to amputate, and finally did so. Morse stood the operation like the hero he was, and we gave him the best care possible under such circumstances. Nevertheless, thirty days later the flesh had receded three inches from the end of the bone, leaving it protruding from the stump. This condition was largely due to the careless and bungling manner in which the operation had been performed. Sloughing of the parts ensued. A piece of flesh as large as the palm of my hand dropped out from alongside the bone, and at the same time an artery gave way. Chancing to be near him at the time, I at once seized the artery and held it until the doctor, who was summoned, arrived. But for this timely discovery poor Morse's life would surely have gone out in a few seconds. Upon his arrival the doctor ordered that the wound be syringed with tincture of iron and a tourniquet applied, but it was found that the patient was too far reduced in strength to endure this. So, for three days and nights we, by alternate reliefs, held the artery. By this time the process of coagulation had put Morse beyond any danger from hemorrhages, and in a short time he recovered sufficiently and was paroled. The last I saw of the brave and courageous Morse was when he was being borne upon a stretcher to the wharf to take passage on a vessel bound for God's country. Now, after the lapse of nearly thirty-five years, it would be a source of the greatest gratification to me to know that this lion-hearted man lived to reach his home in safety; that he did not die in the "southern conthieveracy." I am well assured that his indomitable pluck and will had the power to sustain him until he returned safely home again.

I observed in my intercourse with my prison associates that the brave-hearted, determined fellows were the ones who stood the ravages of starvation and exposure much more successfully than those of a softer, gentler disposition. When one was seen to be despondent and homesick, we at once concluded that the chances were against him. As a matter of fact, these were first to succumb to the effects of the terrible regime. Knowing this, we made all sorts of efforts to cheer each other up by song singing and storytelling. When these diversions failed to arouse a despondent comrade, we generally looked upon his case as hopeless. As a rule we were quite correct in our judgement, for after losing heart the depressed individual usually lived but a brief time. So, to try and prevent any of the boys from falling prey to chronic homesickness, we used to keep up the singing in our frame building, which we occupied as a sleeping room, until late at night. One of our best and happiest singers as I remember it, was a comrade by the name of Paul Graham, who was a resident of the Ligonier Valley. I think he was a member of the Fourth Pennsylvania Cavalry. I never had the pleasure of seeing Graham after the war, but later learned from the postmaster of Ligonier that he had died.

There were many instances of suffering in that hospital which might have been relieved, if not entirely obviated, if the doctors in charge had been as humane and skillful as they ought to have been. One of my patients, a large, robust man, whose name escapes me, was attacked with diphtheria, and was desperately sick. As he had a vigorous constitution, we saw no reason why the patient might not pull through if the proper treatment was given. One evening, shortly after the doctor had made his usual rounds and left the building, the patient was taken worse. I immediately sent for the doctor, but as was usual, a vast amount of circumlocution had to be enacted before a response to the call could be made. So, before the doctor arrived the man was dead. He died in great agony. In fact, of all the deaths which I was called upon while there to witness, his was the most horrific. Then the doctor had assurance to tell me that he could have saved the man's life by an operation. Well knowing the patient's condition, and seeing that an operation would save his life, why did he not perform it at the proper time? There were so many deaths occurring in the ward and so many names now escape me, but I recall that among those who died there were Charles Robinson of Wisconsin and Hiram Hornbeck of New York. I also had one case of scurvy which terminated fatally, the patient being a mass of putrefying sores from the crown of his head to the soles of his feet. This foul disease results from want of proper vegetable food.

About this time the rebels began to fill the places made vacant by death in my ward, by bringing in from Libby enough to fill the cots with her lousy, ragged inmates, who from the treatment they had received, were more dead than alive. Our first care was to free them from the myriads of vermin that infested their meager clothing and preyed upon their poor, emaciated bodies. As soon as we received a recruit from Libby he was stripped naked, washed and put to bed, and his clothes were hung out a window in order that the lice might suffer death from freezing. After a week or two of exposure to the frost, the lice would disappear, and then the clothing would be tied into a bundle and placed under the head of the patient's couch in case the owner of the clothes still had tarried flesh when the louse killing process was ended. If not, which was often the case, some other poor suffering soul got them. I am well aware that it is difficult for persons who have had no opportunity of observing the rapidity of "body vermin" multiplying, to conceive of the condition a person finds himself in shortly after being inflicted with those little brutes. They grow and flourish like a green bay tree, especially if one is hampered in his facilities for fighting them, as all the prisoners of the Confederacy were.

I am inclined to pass over this in silence on account of its repulsiveness, but for the horribly miserable condition of the poor Union prisoners as they came to us at the hospital from Libby. As one object of this narrative is to inform the people about the suffering of our soldiers while confined in the prison pens of the South, I shall offer no further apology. The following is completely true. I frequently received men into the ward whose bodies were literally eaten full of holes by parasites, as though it was not enough that their poor bodies, weakened by starvation, had scarcely vitality sufficient to sustain the spark of life within them. They were also obliged to furnish sustenance to the multitudinous insect life which swarmed and preyed unhindered upon their emaciated frames. Our conflicts with the "graybacks," or body lice, thanks to the freezing process, were not so long drawn or desperate, but when we came to deal with the head lice we were never quite sure when the conflict would end. Our weapons against this enemy were crude and consisted firstly of a comb with teeth, something of the order of a garden rake, which a Yankee prisoner had made from a piece of bone with a pocket knife. Then we had a bit of an old gum-blanket which we utilized as a receptacle for the fallen foe. In addition, we had an old iron kettle. With this armament we waged a war of extermination against these pestiferous parasites. The "modus operandi" resorted to in the case of a man having a heavy head of hair and an unusually thick beard was a process that would shock polite society.

When this patient was brought in from Libby, Ritchie and I took charge of him. After divesting him of his garments, we put him to bed. We then, after allowing him to rest a little, propped him up on his couch and spreading the rubber blanket over his lap, commenced the raking process. The lice would rattle down upon the blanket like falling rain at every passage of the rude comb through his hair. The poor man himself was greatly astonished at the magnitude of the catch, and as he looked upon the constantly increasing pile of live animals, his exclamations of surprise were both amusing and pathetic. This was no marvel, for we actually secured in this particular case about one pint of lice from his head and beard. In following this process we succeeded in ridding our patient of his tormentors, but the operation was prolonged from the fact that every hair in the man's head was covered for at least one inch from the scalp with nits. These pests continued to hatch out, so we were obliged to repeat the bathing with the infusion of tobacco for several days.

The first day of January, 1865, was a day long to be remembered on account of its being so intensely cold at Richmond. The James River froze over its entire width that night, a thing which rarely occurred. "Indeed, it has not happened for twenty years," said Superintendent Woodward. A large number of prisoners in Libby were cruelly frozen during the cold. They were allowed no fire at all, and the windows were entirely open. On the day following I received a contingent of the victims of the frost from Libby and a sorry lot they were. Some of the number had their feet so badly frozen that their toes actually dropped from their feet. This hellish act on the part of the rebels, for a wonder, called out uncomplimentary comments from their own people which resulted in their boarding up the windows, thus leaving the prisoners in perpetual darkness. They were not subjected to a combination of the plagues of intense cold, darkness and lice. I firmly believe that if the hellish rebel authorities could have devised any other plagues they would have been added to those already enumerated.

The tomahawk and scalping knife of the savage, the rack and thumbscrew of the Inquisition, or the nameless barbarities of the Turk are all mild and merciful in comparison with the tortures heaped upon the inmates of the southern prison hells. How could human beings become so heartless and cruel as to let their fellow creatures suffer and die of cold and hunger? The question has been so often asked I beg leave to say that the people of the South generally, if they had been left to follow their own inclinations, would have made the prisoners comfortable. The rebel authorities, however, were maddened by their failure to accomplish by arms in the field their scheme of secession. Having lost all hope of successfully coping with the Yankees in the field, they deliberately devised and put into operation a damnable regime of starvation with all its concomitant horrors. Why such brutalities were allowed by our government to be practiced upon our soldiers, whom the fate of war had thrown into the enemy's hands, I cannot understand. The government had stopped the exchange of prisoners of war, thus enabling the rebels to starve many thousands of our soldiers who otherwise would have been restored to usefulness in our ranks through exchange. The war was not waged on the part of the North primarily for the purpose of abolishing slavery, but it was fought with the sole object of suppressing the rebellion of the slave-holding states. Instead of going at the traitors "hammer and tongs," as any other government on earth would probably have done, our authorities truckled, with honeyed words, hoping to win the recalcitrant states back to their allegiance to the Union at any cost short of its own existence. All this time the uncompromising rebels were scorning every offer of reconciliation, and were practicing all the hellish arts of a refined barbarism to win their cause.

Under the Emancipation Proclamation, if the rebellious states had laid down their arms in a prescribed manner, they could have resumed their standing in the Union and retained their property in human souls. Had they done this, the sum of all villainies would probably exist today in the "land of the free, and the home of the brave," as in the antebellum days. There evidently should have been issued, on the day Fort Sumter was fired upon, a proclamation containing just four words: "Unconditional Surrender or Death!" The war should have been fought on the line, "An eye for an eye, and a tooth for a tooth." I grant you that had this been the case the war would not have dragged on for four years.

It seems strange to me that even our most brilliant statesmen and our wisest philosophers failed to recognize the fact that the cup of iniquity of the slave-holding South was filled to repletion, and that we of the North, who were not wholly guiltless for its continuance, were the chosen instruments of Providence for the wiping from our nation's fair escutcheon the foul blot of human thralldom. Had this underlying fact been recognized from the first, and the war prosecuted with the vigor that would naturally grow out of such a heaven-imposed task, it doubtless would have reached a speedy termination, for our army was composed of as courageous a body of men as ever caused old earth to tremble beneath its martial tread.

Toward the latter part of January, 1865, an exchange of prisoners was arranged for, and our patients were being sent north. Finally, my comrades were all taken away and my ward was closed. I was sent to the floor below for a few days. While here I formed the acquaintance of a patient whose names was John Swihart, and whose home was at Masillon, Ohio. Of all the poor, lean men I had ever seen, John was the thinnest. I think his weight would have fallen under fifty pounds. I used my own person as the standard of measure in such cases, as I had, while in perfect health, been reduced from 170 pounds normal weight, until I tipped the beam of the rebel scales upon which our rations were weighed to us, at just one hundred pounds. So thin was John that I often thought that if his stomach itched he was just as likely to scratch his backbone through it as not.

His condition proved a great puzzle to the rebel doctors who were unable to determine the nature of his malady, as he became thinner and weaker day by day, and yet showed no symptoms of organic disease. His lung power was unimpaired and remained remarkably strong, for one so emaciated as he, and when he took a notion to "yell," as he frequently did, his stentorian voice would wake the echoes throughout the entire building. John would be talking with some comrade or attendant in an ordinary tone of voice, and as intelligently as anyone, when perhaps in the midst of a sentence he would break off and give vent to the most unearthly yells. He screamed, "Ouch! Ouch! Oh, Lord Oh!" Then, resuming the conversation where he had left off, he would talk on as if nothing had happened. John was cared for by a stalwart Michigan cavalryman by the name of King, who nursed him tenderly, and handled him as easily as an ordinary man would have handled a baby. Finally, the Annex to General Hospital Number 21 was closed, and the patients and attendants, with the exception of a New Yorker by the name of Sawyer, and myself, were all paroled. The last I ever saw of the amazing John Swihart was when he was carried on a stretcher toward the boat that was to speed him away to his family home.

Sawyer and myself were now transferred to Hospital Number 21, where I had the "distinguished honor" of being installed wardmaster over a small room on the first floor. Sawyer served as a nurse. This room contained only twenty-eight cots and was reserved for the most desperate cases. At about eight o'clock in the morning the rebels brought to my ward a patient for each cot in the room. They were the toughest, most miserable and pitiful specimens of humanity I ever cast my eyes upon during all my terrible experience with destitution, disease and starvation. None of these patients had received a bath for a month or more and they were smoked until their skins were the color of a smoked ham. Clothed in filthy rags, with skeleton frames and gaunt faces, they were indeed pitiful and distressing objects to behold. We proceeded at once to make the poor creatures as comfortable as was possible under the circumstances.

While we were in the midst of our efforts to make our patients more comfortable and presentable, the rebel doctor came in. He was a gray haired man of some sixty years. His name, I believe, was Doctor Rathburn. I shall never forget the expression of horror which spread over the old doctor's face as he looked upon the desperate condition of these poor wretches. "My God," he exclaimed. "We can do nothing for these men. They will all die. All I can hope to do for them is to make it as easy for them as possible." He then prescribed ten drops of laudanum in a gill of whiskey, three times per day, to each and every patient. Eight of these men expired within four hours of being brought in.

One of these patients was John Barman, with whom I had been well acquainted. He belonged to Company F, Eighth Pennsylvania Reserves, my own regiment. I failed to recognize him at first owing to his blackened and terrible condition. While I was fixing him up as comfortably as I could, he called my name and told me who he was. Grasping his hand, I sat down by him on the cot, while in the weak and trembling voice of a dying man, he told me of the horrible deaths of many of my comrades. They had met their fate in the prison hell of Salisbury, North Carolina. As he mentioned the names of long-loved school friends, messmates and fellow soldiers, who had been swallowed up in that hellish maelstrom of rebel malignity, it seemed to me my heart must break. I gave way to a flood of tears. But they were not the tears of unmingled grief, for indignation claimed her rights. Alas! My poor comrades! Brave heroes of many a hard fought field, was this thy inglorious end? For shame, ungrateful republic! To abandon thy gallant sons to the ignominy of death by starvation, when one act of justifiable retaliation would have saved their valuable lives for the service of our country. I have never been able to see any possible excuse for our authorities failing to demand of the rebels proper treatment of our prisoners of war. This news imparted to me by Barman, concerning the fate of my old comrades at Salisbury, was the first tidings I had received of them since my escape from the boxcar. So depressed was I by his narration that I was greatly dejected for several days thereafter. Poor Barman soon responded to the last roll call, and was mustered out of the earthly ranks to join the great majority of our comrades on the eternal camping grounds above.

As no clothing was allowed to remain on a corpse, Sawyer removed the ragged habiliments from Barman's body, and covering it with a sheet, he and I carried it to a building across the way which was used as a dead house. Oh, my God! What a horrible sight was presented here for our view! I cannot think of it even to this day without a feeling of horror, for there on the floor lay sixteen corpses, perfect skeletons, stark naked, with eyes, noses and mouths all eaten away by the rats. The eyeless sockets, missing noses and grinning teeth of those poor bodies made such a scene of gruesome, horrible reality as was never conceived of even by the morbid imagination of Dante. Summon, oh Satan, from the remotest regions of gloomy hades and expend thy hellish vocabulary of hate to shower statements of deep damnation on the heads of those who planned and perpetrated such fiendish mutilation upon brave and noble men!

The dead-cart was purposely allowed to make but one trip each twenty-four hours, so that those dying after the cart man had made his round could be left in the dead house to fatten the rats until the next day. These rats, like the vultures on the towers of silence among the Hindus of India, from long usage had become adept at their ghastly work. They attacked only the eyes, noses and lips of their victims until these were exhausted. As the supply of new corpses was always equal to the demand, the rats fed on these "dainties" constantly. Now this hideous mutilation could have been prevented by having the cart conveying the dead make two trips daily, and allowing the bodies of those dying after the last trip to lie on the cots until the following morning, or until the cart came around again. But this would not have so fully gratified the rebel desire to heap indignities upon the Yankee dead. The rat-eaten dead were thrown indiscriminantly into the cart, like so many logs of wood. A tarpaulin was stretched over them and they were hauled out through the streets of Christian Richmond and consigned to a ditch and covered slightly with earth. They were then left there with names unknown and unrecorded, to molder back to dust. Thus was their identity cruelly obliterated.

This was the fate of every Union soldier who died at General Hospital Number 21, at Richmond, Virginia, during the several months of my sojourn there. Brave defenders of an ungrateful republic! Thou has sealed thy devotion to thy country's cause by a martyr's death. Thy name hast been stricken from the annals of earth as though thou hadst never lived, but thy memory shall remain green in the hearts of thy surviving comrades until the Grim Reaper summons us to the eternal shore!

Chapter Fifteen

DOOM OF THE CONFEDERACY

Among my patients was an Irishman named Patrick Kane. He was a member of the Seventh Regulars. Kane was suffering from dropsy and although too much reduced from the combined effects of disease and starvation to stand upon his feet, or even to sit up, he remained incredibly pugnacious. He was always ready to fight everybody and everything in sight. Pat's cot was located in the center of the ward. If Sawyer, the nurse, did not give him the first slice of corn bread cut from the loaf when he distributed rations, Kane would fire his piece at the former's head.

Pat finally made up his mind that he would take no more medicine. He would at times pretend to take it by holding it in his mouth and then squirting it out over the other patients. The doctor told me to hold the patient's nose and make him swallow his medicine. I did so, and when he found out that I was determined to make him behave himself, he became despondent. Although his condition continued to seemingly improve, Pat continued his growling. One morning soon after making him take his remedies, I said to him, "Well, Pat, how are you this morning?" "Oh, Jasus," said he. "I'm going to die tonight!" "Oh, you're all right," I said. "You're getting stronger everyday." The following morning I said to him, "Well, Pat, I see you didn't die last night after all." He then smote his breast with his fist and said, "Be Jasus, if I don't die tonight, divil a bit will I die at all, at all." Pat didn't die that night and it wasn't long before he was paroled. I have every reason to believe he lived to reach God's country once more.

There was partitioned off of the end of my ward a little room which Sawyer and myself used as a sort of storeroom for medicines and any extra rations which might chance to fall into our hands. It was fitted with a bench which extended across one end of it, and underneath it was boxed off into small compartments. As the majority of my patients were in such physical condition as to be unable to eat the rough food supplied by the rebels, I sometimes had an accumulation of rations from this source. I was able to add to this, from time to time, a little from my own wardmaster's full allowance. From this surplus under the bench I was often enabled to carry and distribute food to the men in the other wards who were in a condition to eat. But I was very careful not to let the rebels catch me at it, for if I had been detected in sharing my rations with the starving, I would probably have been hustled off to Libby as a punishment.

The building in which our hospital was located, had, prior to the war, been used to manufacture tobacco. The brand of tobacco produced there was known as "The Conqueror." There were large numbers of circulars strewn about the place, upon which the picture of an armored knight with plumed helmet and a drawn sword standing over his fallen foe was printed. Some Yank, having secured two of these circulars, cut from them the pictures and printed under them the following apt lines: "He that taketh up the sword shall perish by the sword," and "The sword is my inheritance, let tyrants tremble." He then pasted them on the wall of the prison. For some reason, they were left undisturbed by the Johnnies; and as the collapse of the Confederacy soon followed, it almost seems as if those quotations were prophetic.

Despondency seemed to settle like a thick pall, over the hopes of the rebels with the news of George B. McClellan's defeat in the 1864 presidential election. As the Confederacy tottered to its end the desire of many rebels to kill and destroy seemed rather to intensify in hellishness. As their hopes of success grew even less, the Confederacy lay prone and helpless, like a huge serpent, in impotent rage. In a final act of senseless brutality the rebs began to destroy their capital city of Richmond.

By 1865, it cost one thousand Confederate dollars for a suit of very ordinary clothes. Five hundred rebel dollars purchased a barrel of flour. One hundred of their dollars got a cord of wood. One rebel dollar bought a loaf of bread weighing no more than five ounces, or, perhaps, a clay pipe. Fifty of their cents bought a block of matches. Onions could be had for one Confederate dollar each. But a dollar in greenbacks would purchase forty dollars in Confederate currency. It was amusing to observe with what aviditiy the Johnnies would gobble up the few greenbacks which came their way, even at the disparity of forty to one, thus showing their lack of confidence in their own government. Indeed, about this time I witnessed Mr. Woodward, the superintendent of the hospital, twist up a twenty dollar blueback to light his cigar.

It was now about the middle of March, 1865, and General Hospital Number 21, began to pass out of existence with the ebbing tide of rebellion. The greater number of the patients had already been paroled, and none were then being received. Sawyer and I anxiously awaited for our release to finally arrive. I had been suffering for some six weeks from a peculiar and distressing disease called by the doctors the "Confederate itch." This circumstance greatly added to my desire to go home. I well knew that I could never recover from my malady under the rebel regime, and as my comrades had all been released, the loss of their companionship worried me greatly. The itch proved to be a skin disease which made its appearance in the form of small, watery pimples no larger than a pin-head. It confined its attack to the breast, hands, and the insides of the arms and legs. The pimples came out in myriads, close together, and were so excruciatingly itchy, especially if the sufferer approached a fire, as to become unbearable. Scratching only served to exaggerate the suffering and to forbear scratching was almost impossible. It simply became "Scratch Yank, or die." Finally, when the disease had expended its force on one particular spot, the rheum would dry up, the skin became indurated and flakes scaled off. It was several years before I was rid of the worst of this disease, but even twenty years later it would occasionally make its rude appearance upon my person.

On March 23, 1865, the auspicious moment came and Sawyer and myself were, with the few others remaining, paroled. I think we were the last squad of Federal prisoners to be exchanged. About ten days later Richmond was captured. Words are inadequate to express the happiness and joy we experienced when at last we turned our backs upon that detestable city of misery, starvation and death. With glad exultation we marched down to the wharf and boarded the rebel flag-of-truce boat to sail us back to the sheltering folds of "Old Glory" once more. Farewell my dead comrades! A long farewell! Peacefully sleep, quietly rest, though it be in the unhallowed soil of a traitorous Virginia.

No more shall war's rude alarms burst upon your devoted ears. No more shall an ungrateful country call you as a bootless sacrifice to the unholy ambitions of false and incompetent chieftains. Sleep in peace.

Our boat backed away from her moorings, and we steamed away down the James to the outpost of the rebel lines, where we were met by a Union vessel to which we were transferred. At last we were beneath the starry folds of the banner of the free. Out of the depths of perdition's cell. Free from the jaws of death; extricated from the mouth of hell itself.

It was indeed a pathetic spectacle to see those poor, miserably starved men, clothed in filthy rags, raise their weak voices to cheer at the sight of the old flag. Tears of joy and gratitude ran like torrents down our cheeks. We were soon on our way to Fortress Monroe, which we reached in the evening, and after a short stay we crossed the bay to Annapolis, Maryland. The day had been cold and raw. As night came on the Chesapeake became frosty. As the boat could furnish neither blankets nor overcoats, we were obliged to lie out on deck in the open air with no covering of any sort. Because of this, several of the boys perished in the night from exposure to the elements. They were discovered in the morning with their glassy eyes staring up from the deck to the masthead, where floated the flag they loved so well. And thus, on the very threshold of freedom, and so near to friends and home, they died, victims of someone's wretched carelessness.

We finally arrived at Annapolis and were quartered in the barracks designed for the use of returned prisoners. Upon our arrival, we were stripped to the buff, given a bath, furnished with a completely new uniform and two month's pay. As I had received no pay for almost two years, this money was highly acceptable to me and I was able to purchase a few dainties and knickknacks. Sawyer's solicitude also seemed largely centered on his stomach, and upon receiving his pay, he said he would have a full meal. A peddler came along at this point and sold him a lot of food. The peddler's wares consisted of hard-boiled eggs with salt and pepper for dressing. Sawyer ate twenty-six of those eggs! The peddler's eyes were distended in surprise, especially after the disappearance of the first dozen, but as he had evidently struck a bonanza in Sawyer's insatiable appetite, he offered no objections. I was alarmed for Sawyer's safety, but my pleas were in vain. I told him that such a gorge would kill him. His reply was, that if it did, he would at least die with the satisfaction of a full stomach! Strangely, Sawyer suffered no noticeable ill effects from his reckless indulgence in hard-boiled eggs. A few days later, Sawyer and I parted company, never to meet again on the shores of time.

The camp itself was an uninviting spot. As a returned prisoner, I was invariably anxious to get home to my loving family. The long absence from loved ones and the terrible suffering I'd endured in southern prisons, made me long for home. The immense heaps of cast off shoes and clothing, crawling with graybacks, which accumulated there, served as a constant reminder of my recent prison ordeal. It was scarcely possible to realize that I was once more a free man.

I had the good fortune to meet my old comrade, James W. Eberhart, there in the fort. We had not seen each other since the day upon which we left the inferno at Belle Isle to be transferred to the hell at Salisbury. Eberhart was terribly reduced in flesh, was sick and weak and virtually lost his voice. Needless to say, our comradeship was resumed. We ate and slept in the same barracks. He had been paroled from Salisbury a month before I was at Richmond, but the rebels had sent him by the way of Raleigh, causing many delays, so that he was nearly a month in reaching Annapolis. He occupied a bunk directly over mine in the barracks and one night while in a trance, he fell out of bed and was stunned by the fall. On being carried out into the air and revived, his voice suddenly returned to him as good as ever!

Among the rank and file composing a company of American volunteers may be found men of such sterling qualities of both head and heart as to command the respect and admiration of an entire company. Such a man was Sergeant James W. Eberhart, of Company G. Generous, kindhearted and uncomplaining, he cheerfully performed any duty assigned him, however arduous or dangerous it may have been. Brave and courageous at all times, yet so gentle and kind to all, Jim never aroused the ire of anyone. His grandfather was a patriotic soldier during the "times that tried men's souls," at Valley Forge, and the grandson was not a whit behind the grandsire in soldierly qualities during the war of the Great Rebellion. He was dubbed "Pedee," and he was universally known as Pedee throughout the war.

Pedee, who was a member of my mess, was an inveterate smoker, and after taking his noonday smoke would always lie down for a nap when off duty. We had been supplied with waterproof cartridges which were enclosed in a glazed film. These films were highly explosive and one day while Pedee was sleeping, I emptied his half-smoked, short-stemmed pipe of its contents and inserting one of these films in the bottom, replaced the tobacco on top of it. After his nap was over Pedee reached for his pipe and lit it. He then sat himself down for a nice quiet smoke. Suddenly there was a swish, and the pipe dropped to the floor, while the contents went sailing up his nose. His snorting, sneezing and coughing drew forth shouts of laughter from the boys at first, as they all expected him to get furious, tear around and threaten to wipe up the ground with the noodle-headed imbecile who pulled this measly trick. But he did nothing of the kind. After the paroxysm of sneezing was over, without saying a word, he picked up his old dudeen, loaded it to the brim with fresh tobacco, lit up, and sat down for a placid smoke as usual. Ninety-nine out of one hundred men would have been fighting mad, but Pedee was always in complete control of his emotions. I never saw him show excitement even under the most dangerous or aggravating of circumstances.

In Salisbury, that hell-hole of misery, starvation and death, Pedee was the Good Samaritan. He visited the hospital cheering the despairing and relieving the misery of the sick and dying. Although starving himself, with a sublime devotion, and a self-abnegation unequalled, he deprived himself of bread rations so that he might make poultices from those whose desperate sufferings were greater than even his own. He was attacked by scurvy and his teeth dropped one by one from his jaws. He lost all power of speech, which, however, was miraculously recovered after his release from prison. He remained throughout the same kind, congenial and uncomplaining man he had always been.

My messmates were all good men and true, but the qualities of Sturgis and Eberhart seemed to leave a more lasting impression on me than the others.

The three left flank companies of the regiment, B, G, and K, naturally became friendly and quite social. We entered into one another's sports and became acquainted with individual members. Company K had two unique members, of whom one was called "Groundhog" and the other "Pig-Tracks." The former was a singular looking man with a heavy reddish beard and derived his name from the fact that he endeavored to burrow into the ground for protection in our first battle, and it would make him very wrathful to shout "Groundhog" at him. It is safe to say we all became groundhogs and gophers before the war was ended. The other man received his euphonious title from the fact that whenever he got filled up on commissary whisky, he would go about shouting "Pig-Tracks" in the most unaccountable manner. Like "Groundhog" he resented his name, and for this reason the names stuck to them throughout their service.

Eberhart left for home several days before I did. I was taken violently ill on the train ride home with bronchitis. Upon arriving at Harrsburg, I was so weak that I had to lie on the station platform until the train arrived for Pittsburgh. I finally reached my home in Uniontown, Pennsylvania, and after being confined to bed for three weeks, I recovered sufficiently to rejoin my command at Arlington Heights, Virginia, after they had returned from Richmond. I was mustered out with my regiment and discharged in Harrisburg after four years, two months and eleven days of continuous active service.

And the Star Spangled Banner in triumph shall wave
O'er the land of the free and the home of the brave.

Chapter Sixteen

SALISBURY

The Confederate prison at Salisbury, North Carolina, became notorious on account of the diabolical tortures which were perpetrated there upon Union prisoners. It is truly humiliating for me, as a veteran of the Army of the Potomac, to record that here at this prison, brave, patriotic men were subject to barbarous and inhuman treatment by fellow Americans. I blush with shame for my countrymen, when for truth and history's sake, I am obliged to record the savage treatment meted out to helpless men by those who were in armed rebellion against our government. The bald fact remains that the sufferings to which we, as prisoners of war, were subject were inflicted coolly, deliberately, and with incredible malice.

Everything was done by our government to render Confederate prisoners of war the utmost in kindness and consideration. Everything was done to render their captivity as little galling to them as possible. They were provided with clean, comfortable quarters, where sanitary conditions were readily obtainable. They were provided with comfortable clothing and supplied with an abundance of food. Particular care was always exercised by our government to locate their camps of detention where an abundance of fresh water was obtainable. In addition, to all these arrangements and conditions for the health and comfort of the rebel prisoners, there were always in attendance sufficient doctors for the wounded and sick and the best of medical and surgical care. Great care and tenderness was shown them throughout the war.

Rebel apologists have attempted to create a diversion from the fact that Confederate authorities did treat prisoners of war with hellish cruelty, by asserting that their soldiers, held also as prisoners in the North, were also treated with such barbarity, but in clear and complete refutation of this charge is the historic fact that the rate of mortality among the rebel prisoners confined in the North was more than fifty percent less than among Union prisoners held in the South. Most of these Union men were starved to death, or were so far reduced in strength by an emaciation purposely inflicted for the securing of a traitorous end. Our boys fell easy prey to sickness and disease. They were swept away in great numbers. It is doubtless difficult for an average person to conceive of the horrors experienced at Salisbury. Human language utterly fails to furnish words with which to faithfully paint the pictures of suffering and distress which our brave boys were called to pass through as prisoners of war in the pens of the South.

After being divested of all possessions and with nothing to cover their nakedness but their undergarments, many men were left to shiver and suffer from exposure for the frosts of the fall and winter. A regime of starvation was practiced at Salisbury which was carried on to completion. I think that the arch fiend himself would have been hard pressed to devise a more horrible means of torture and death than was common practice at Salisbury. Without question it would have been more merciful to have withheld food entirely to allow the victims to die in a relatively short period of time, than to have pursued the course of slow starvation.

The rebels would serve us with something called a "cob meal." They knew that there was no nutrition in a corncob, and they also knew that a human being could only live for a few months even if fed upon bread made from corn, ground cob and all. Therefore the tactic of killing off the prisoners more efficiently through this corncob meal was invented and introduced with hellish ingenuity. The poor, weak, half-starved creatures compelled to eat this bread were often attacked by a violent diarrhoea which in a weakened condition would become acute. It would then become chronic and in a short time the victim would suffer a terrible death. This was surely an effectual means of converting live Yankees into dead ones.

Captain Davis of a New York regiment was shot by a guard when he was not near the deadline. This was another of their favorite methods of making dead Yankees and many innocent inoffensive prisoners were thus brutally murdered. A thirty day furlough was given to the murderer as a reward.

Enough can never be said about the brutal rebel regime at the Salisbury, North Carolina, prison camp. Hundreds of men, survivors of this ghastly place, would attest to the truth of my statements. Of those who survived Salisbury most returned home in a near skeletal state and would never be fully able-bodied again. About half of the Pennsylvania boys imprisoned there from the fall of 1864 until the spring of 1865, died a miserable death and were buried in a mass grave. Sleep on, brave heroes, neither storied urn nor animated bust may ever mark the unknown, unhonored ditch which swallowed up your fleeting clay, but your suffering and heroism will never be forgotten.

Chapter Seventeen

RETROSPECTIVE

Cavaliers, falsifiers, and perjurers, have for many years since the Civil War resorted to every dishonorable, false and despicable means to explain, excuse, and deny the horrible and deliberate starvation of Union prisoners of war. The facts and figures are true and unanswerable, and from my own experience as a "rebel soldier" in the Soldier's Retreat at Richmond, I positively know they had good and sufficient food to dispense. The truth of this statement is amply proven by the fact that no rebel soldier was ever known to starve to death, and yet according to these liars the Yankee prisoners of war were being fed the same quantity and quality of food as were the rank and file in the rebel army. This same rebel army, although fed upon the same kind of food upon which many thousands of Union prisoners starved to death, were capable of prosecuting and conducting active and vigorous campaigns throughout the entire war.

To prove that the starvation of Union prisoners was deliberately planned and executed, is the fact that of all the food and clothing sent to the prisoners from the North none of it was ever issued to them and they were allowed to die in agony, with their starved eyes resting upon the very building containing this food. In the two hundred and thirty-two battles of the Civil War, over forty-nine thousand Federals were killed upon the field in action. In the prison hells of the South over seventy-one thousand brave, patriotic martyrs suffered a lingering death in their country's cause.

"Cease guns, be still; one day is set
Which strife nor battle mars,
For souls that in their cloudy tents
Are camping near the stars.

Some forms on lofty hilltops rest,
Some in the valleys lie;

> The tropic grasses wave o'er some,
> O'er some the waters sigh.
>
> Rank, line and file forever more
> Shall dream of glory proud,
> While floats the flag they carried far,
> And gathered for a shroud."

What I have written in these pages is the complete truth as I have the ability to fathom it. I have written about the things I saw and experienced firsthand, the things that have been and always shall be true, conscious of right, and fearing no wrong.

APPENDIX A

The Eighth Regiment, Pennsylvania Reserve Volunteer Corps
(37th Volunteers)

1861-1864

---

1. Organized at Pittsburgh in July, 1861.

2. Ordered to Washington D.C., July 30, 1861; attached to First Brigade, McCall's Pennsylvania Reserves Division, Army of the Potomac, until March, 1862.

3. Duty at Tennallytown, Maryland, August 2, 1861, until October 10, 1861, and at Camp Pierpont, near Langley, Virginia, until March, 1862.

4. Skirmish at Great Falls on September 4, 1861.

5. Advance on Manassas, Virginia, March 10-15, 1862.

6. Attached to First Brigade, Second Division, First Army Corps, Army of the Potomac, March-April, 1862.

7. McDowell's advance on Falmouth, Virginia, April 9-19, 1862.

8. Attached to First Brigade, McCall's Division, Department of the Rappahannock, April-June, 1862; also, Second Brigade, Second Division, Department of the Rappahannock until June, 1862.

9. Duty at Fredericksburg, Virginia, until June, 1862.

10. Moved to the White House, June 9-11, 1862.

11. Seven days before Richmond, June 25-July 1, 1862.

12. Battle of Mechanicsville, June 26, 1862.

13. Battle of Gaines' Mill, June 27, 1862.

14. Battles of Charles City Crossroads and Glendale, Virginia, June 30, 1862.

15. Battle of Malvern Hill, July 1, 1862.

16. At Harrison's Landing, Virginia, until August 16, 1862.

17. Attached to the Second Brigade, Third Division, Fifth Army Corps, Army of the Potomac, until August, 1862; and then, Second Brigade, Third Division, Third Army Corps, Army of Virginia, until September, 1862.

18. Movement to join General Pope, August 16-26, 1862.

19. Battle of Gainesville, August 28, 1862.

20. Battle of Groveton, August 29, 1862.

21. Second Battle of Bull Run, August 30, 1862.

22. The Maryland Campaign, September 6-24, 1862.

23. Battle of South Mountain, Maryland, September 14, 1862.

24. Battle of Antietam, September 16-17, 1862.

25. Attached to the Second Brigade, Third Division, First Army Corps, Army of the Potomac, until February, 1862.

26. Duty in Maryland until October, 1862.

27. Movement to Falmouth, Virginia, October 30-November 19, 1862.

28. Battle of Fredericksburg, December 12-15, 1862.

29. The "Mud March," January 20-24, 1863.

30. Ordered to Washington D.C., February 6, 1863.

31. Attached to the Second Brigade, Pennsylvania Reserves Corps, Twenty-Second Corps, Department of Washington until April, 1863, also the District of Alexandria, Twenty-Second Corps, until April, 1864.

32. Duty in Washington D.C., and also at Alexandria, Virginia, until April, 1864.

33. Attached to the Third Brigade, Third Division, Fifth Army Corps, Army of the Potomac, until May, 1864.

34. The Rapidan Campaign, May, 1864.

35. Battles of the Wilderness, Virginia, May 5-7, 1864.

36. Battle of Laurel Hill, Virginia, May 8, 1864.

37. The Spotsylvania Campaign, May 8-17, 1864.

38. Assault on the Salient, May 12, 1864.

39. Left the front, May 17, 1864.

40. Mustered out, May 24, 1864.

The regiment lost during active service five officers and 153 enlisted men killed or mortally wounded. Another sixty-eight enlisted men died of disease. Total dead: 226 men.

APPENDIX B

The 191st Pennsylvania Infantry

1864-1865

1. Organized in the field from Veterans and Recruits of the Pennsylvania Reserve Corps, May 31, 1864.

2. Attached to the Third Brigade, Third Division, Fifth Army Corps, Army of the Potomac, until August, 1864; and then, the First Brigade, Third Division, Fifth Army Corps, Army of the Potomac, until September, 1864.

3. Battles about Cold Harbor, Virginia, June 1-12, 1864.

4. Battle of Bethesda Church, Virginia, June 1-3, 1864.

5. Battle of White Oak Swamp Bridge, Virginia, June 13, 1864.

6. Before Petersburg, Virginia, June 16-18, 1864.

7. Siege of Petersburg, June 16, 1864, until April 2, 1865.

8. At Weldon Railroad, Virginia, June 21-23, 1864.

9. The Mine Explosion, Petersburg, Virginia, July 30, 1864.

10. At Weldon Railroad, Virginia, August 18-21, 1864.

11. Attached to the Third Brigade, Second Division, Fifth Army Corps, Army of the Potomac, until June, 1865.

12. Poplar Springs Church, Virginia, September 29-October 2, 1864.

13. At Boydton Plank Road and Hatcher's Run, Virginia, October 27-28, 1864.

14. ` Warren's Expedition to the Weldon Railroad, December 7-12, 1864.

15. At Dabney's Mills and Hatcher's Run, February 5-7, 1865.

16. The Appomattox Campaign, March 28-April 9, 1865.

17. At Lewis Farm, near Gravelly Road, Virginia, March 29, 1865.

18. At White Oak Road, Virginia, March 31, 1865.

19. At Five Forks, Virginia, April 1, 1865.

20. Before Appomattox Courthouse, Virginia, April 9, 1865; surrender of General Lee and his army.

21. March to Washington D.C., May 1-12, 1865.

22. Participated in the Grand Review in Washington D.C., May 23, 1865.

23. Mustered out, June 28, 1865.

The regiment lost during active service one officer and forty enlisted men killed or mortally wounded. Another 161 enlisted men died of disease. Total dead: 202 men.

APPENDIX C

Private C. H. Golden's Experience

I was a Private during the Civil War. I enlisted as a recruit in the Eighth Regiment, Pennsylvania Reserves and was taken to Camp Copeland, near Pittsburgh (Braddock's field), in January, 1864. I was detailed as a second clerk in the quartermaster's office. Joseph R. Harrah, the first clerk, was also there and was a Sergeant in the 140th Regiment of Pennsylvania Volunteers.

On May 31, 1864, I requested the post commandant and quartermaster to relieve me from duty and return me to my regiment. The commander of the post refused to grant my request. I then and there resolved to go to my regiment without their permission, and made my way from Camp Copeland to near Petersburg, Virginia, and there found Company H, of the 191st Pennsylvania. About the first of June, all the veterans and recruits of the reserve regiments were consolidated into two regiments, known respectively as the 190th and the 191st Pennsylvania Volunteers. These two regiments formed the Third Brigade, in the Third Division, Fifth Army Corps, G. R. Warren commanding. As I commenced the narration of my prison life during that summer while in front of a vigilant enemy about Petersburg, I will confine myself to this subject.

On the 14th of August, the Fifth Corps marched out from the front line before Lee's army and about noon struck the Weldon Railroad at Ream's Station. Our regiment did not tear up the track, but we did the fighting while others of our corps destroyed the railroad for several miles. As we held on to the road, we pushed on toward the south and rear of Petersburg. But the Confederates saw the danger and were at their old flanking movement. Taking a road unknown to our commander they came suddenly upon us, taking a Maryland brigade in the flank and hurling it back. We arrested the charge, however, repelled the Confederates, and fortifying our position, held the Weldon Railroad at last. The usual slow movements nearly proved disastrous to Warren. He was without support, and at a distance from the rest of the army.

The space between should have been filled by General Bragg. Our corps commander ordered him to occupy it. Before Bragg could comply with this order Hill charged forth striking our brigade on the flank and rear, capturing 2,500 men, including about one regiment of the Second Brigade. These men were all from Crawford's division.

We were hurried from the field into the south side of Petersburg, but a few of our men or officers made their escape. We were rolled up as it were, doubled back, which crushed the two brigades. A sadder looking lot of men never entered the Confederacy than we. As the rebel guards marched us through the streets of Petersburg, we were cursed and abused to such an extent that we could hardly stand it. Women and little boys ran along and threw stones at us. It had been raining and the streets themselves were full of muddy water. The boys threw muddy water in our faces. Women from fine houses ran at us with fiendish faces and demonic yells. They would scream, "Grant is taking Petersburg. The old butcher!" A rebel officer on horseback dashed up to me, grabbed my hat, and threw me his old, lousy one in its place.

We were marched over a small bridge to an island in the Appomattox River. We were ordered to remain there. A heavy guard was placed over us during the night of the 16th of August. As soon as I discovered that all hope of escape during the night had been cut off, A. J. Bissett, my messmate, and I lay down to sleep. It would have been pleasant indeed to lose ourselves in grateful unconsciousness in our unfortunate condition for a short time, but I found it impossible to do so. Although weary in body my mind was in a disturbed condition. After darkness enveloped the camp, we found to our sorrow that the camp was not only guarded by thieves, but was alive with them. We used every precaution in hiding our belongings under our bodies, for the rebels had already taken our blankets and overcoats. After tying our shoe strings in hard knots we lay down to rest. Finally, nature overcame me and I fell into a deep sleep. Thieves found us and they began trying to steal our boots, but only succeeded in making off with my quart tin cup. I grieved over the loss of this valuable utensil during my long imprisonment.

On the 17th of August we awoke to the beautiful orb of day risen high above the earth. All was astir in the camp and without an apology for not feeding us the rebs marched us to the cars. Every mother's son was provided with free transportation to Richmond, Virginia, the capital of the Confederacy. We arrived there late in the evening and were hurried from the cars to the Pemberton building. After being accounted for by the proprietor for one night's lodging, we tried to get some sleep. We talked of home, Greene County, Pennsylvania, and all the good things. The morning dawned again and found us without anything to eat. This was our first Sunday in the Confederacy. We were soon called out into the street of the city and marched up along the canal to a building which was in appearance like a state penitentiary, and as we were halted in front of this mammoth place, a terrible wail went up from our ranks. From the throat of one soldier who had been there before was heard the plain word, "Libby!"

We were ordered into two ranks, filed left and marched. As no one preceded us we ran up against the brick walls of that historic prison. This day was the Jewish Sabbath and many of us who were there will never forget it. In this place we were called up in line and searched a second time for money and valuables. The two men who entered the room were rebel officers and said to be of "Hinglish" origin, don't you know. At any rate they were expert thieves. The rebels with a malignity that would disgrace a South Sea heathen, dropped on the floor pictures of our dear ones and stamped them to pieces. The boys were livid with rage and indignation, but we were powerless to prevent it. The rebs took everything we had with the exception of the clothes on our backs. Near noon we received our first ration since capture. We ate it all at one meal. We were issued a loaf of bread as large as a man's fist, made of cornmeal. It weighed about four ounces. With it was given a piece of meat weighing two ounces. We always selected one of our non-commissioned officers to draw and divide the rations. The sergeant would say to each man, "Who's this?" The caller would answer with his name. My first ration of meat was the eyeball of a beef's head. As I had gone forty-eight hours with no food the physical overcame the intellectual and I consumed my rations.

The number of prisoners confined in Libby prison at any one time was never very large, but this was owing solely to the fact that its capacity was limited. We called it "standing room only." Large numbers were confined there temporarily and then transferred to the foul prison holes further south. The total number of unwilling guests reached up into the thousands. Notwithstanding the discomforts and deprivations of the prisoners and the almost total lack of hospital service, the death rate, although large, never approached that of many other prison pens, notably Andersonville, Belle Isle, Millen and Salisbury. Hundreds of brave men died there in abject squalor and wretchedness. Hundreds died after their release from the effect of rebel brutality, while a few of us survived, living witnesses to the martyrdom which well nigh wrecked our tortured bodies. We remained but a few days in this prison, for Libby was overflowing with prisoners. Many more were arriving from beyond the Weldon Railroad and from the Second Corps. In a few days we were all called out of the Libby prison and formed into four ranks. Many of the boys sang, "Tramp! Tramp!" and "John Brown's Body." We thought we were going home. But alas! We were marched off, over and through the Tredegar Ironworks to Belle Isle.

Belle Isle's name now sends a thrill of horror through my very being, as well as to thousands of hearts. Those who suppose that Libby prison witnessed all the horrors of the Southern captivity must learn that a still lower depth of suffering is yet possible.

Belle Isle is a small island in the James River, which, as viewed from a little distance, has enough pretensions of beauty to justify its name. A portion of the island consists of a bluff covered with trees, but the part used as a prison pen was low, sandy and barren, without a tree to protect it from the rays of the sun. The Belle Isle prison pen was an enclosure of some four or five acres, surrounded by an earthwork several feet high, with a ditch on either side. On the edge of the outer ditch guards were stationed all around the enclosure at intervals of forty feet. The interior of the enclosure had some resemblance at a distance to an encampment, a number of low tents being set in regular rows. Close inspection revealed the fact that the tents were old, rotten and torn. At best they could have sheltered only a small percentage of the prisoners. Within these low tents were huddled from fourteen to sixteen thousand men at one time in September. We were not housed up in walls, nor buried in dungeons, but simply turned into the field like so many animals, to find shelter when and how we might. So crowded were we that if each man had lain down on the ground, occupying the generous allotment of a "hospital grave," say seven feet by two, the whole area of the enclosure would have been covered. Here thousands of us lay from the 18th of August 1864, until the 8th of October, with naught but the sky for a covering and sand for a bed. When the hot glare of the summer sun fell upon the oozing morasses of the James, covering its stagnant pools with green slime, we prayed in vain for rain at night, that our fevered bodies might be dipped in the stream beyond. But no, we were forced to broil and bake under the tropical rays of a midday sun, or huddled together like cattle throughout the livelong night in pouring rain storms. Some of us burrowed in the sand, while others scooped out a shallow ditch long and wide enough to receive their bodies, and covering it with brush, made a temporary refuge. When the rain descended they were forced to abandon this haven of rest.

What can I say of the food? It was worse than that at Libby prison and there was less of it. No man in God's country ever fed his swine on such swill. A fragment of corn bread, perhaps half ground, containing cob, husk and all; meat, often tainted, very mule-like, and only a mouthful at that; a tablespoon of rotten beans; soup thin and briny with worms floating on top. Not all these luxuries were had at once, only one at a time, and that in quantity insufficient to support a child of four years. As the weary days and nights dragged on, hunger told its inevitable tale on all; diarrhoea, scurvy, low malarial fevers and lung diseases set in. The poor captives became emaciated and weak. Many could not walk; when they attempted it, giddiness and blindness came on and they fell in their tracks. I shall never forget, during the month of September, I became weak from exposure and the eating of unwholesome food that for three weeks I could not straighten myself. The prisoners were turned out everyday on the other part of the island, and guarded while the enclosure was being cleaned up, after which we would be marched back in four ranks, and counted into the enclosure. I was one of the prisoners in the rear of the column and too weak to keep up. A rebel sergeant of the guards became infuriated with me and grabbing a musket out of another guard's hand, struck and felled me to the ground. Some of my comrades tenderly carried me into the enclosure and restored me to consciousness.

To add to all this misery there came unavoidable consequences from being herded and crowded together. Lice were in all quarters. The bodies of prisoners were encrusted with dirt and vermin. They were sore from lying in the sand and some were lice-eaten to such an extent that hardly a healthy patch of skin was visible. All manner of rumors would originate from the rebels who had charge of us, especially the officers. We did not think it could be possible that our enemies could find a more terrible place than the one we were leaving, but then we did not know anything of the horrors of Salisbury, and it was fortunate for us we did not. That this horrible future was hidden from us prevented many from giving up in utter despair. It was only the continuous hope of a speedy release that enabled us to live through it.

On the 8th of October we were marched from Belle Isle prison out through the Tredegar Ironworks and on over into Manchester, a town directly opposite Richmond where we were loaded on the cars as so much inanimate freight. At seven o'clock p.m., we started on our long journey for Salisbury, North Carolina. We did not know at the time where we were going, but from what we learned from the guards, we supposed our next prison would be somewhere in the far south. We were placed in and on top of freight cars. The first night, between Richmond and Danville, Virginia, the suffering was more than I had ever witnessed. There was great suffering from diarrhoea, stomach cramps and unquenchable thirst. At last morning came. We had reached the city of Danville, about one hundred and forty miles from Richmond. We changed cars at this place, and comrade James M. Seals, of my company, begged a large ear of corn, and burned it at the fire where the railroad men were drying sand. I ate this burnt corn during the day and felt much better. We were ordered aboard the cars. Again A. J. Bissett and I were on top of a boxcar with other prisoners. We remained there all day, and oh, how cold that wind was upon us, without blanket or overcoat, only thin cotton pants, short coat, and those in desperately lousy rags. As the darkness of night was closing above us the train stopped. We had reached a place called Salisbury, North Carolina, and this was to be our home and hell.

I was so very cold and stiff I had to be helped from the train and into the prison. We had by this time found out that Salisbury was to be our place of imprisonment and various were the conjectures as to what kind of place it was and what kind of treatment we'd receive. Surely in our case it was "ignorance was bliss." We were informed by some of the guards that it was a camp in the woods and that alone made the impression that it would be a better place than prison life in a building like Libby or Belle Isle. The description we received of the place was not unfavorable, and the rebels assured us that the treatment we would receive would be much better than that which we received at Richmond. Whether they did this from ignorance, or from a desire to keep the truth from us until they had us safely enclosed in the pen, or from a fiendish desire to increase our torture by disappointment, we could not find out. But we did discover that they were liars or ignorant of what they were talking about, and that all our former experiences and suffering in rebel prisons were but an intimation of what was still in store for us.

> "But that I am forbid
> To tell the secrets of my prison-house
> I could a tale unfold, whose lightest word
> Would harrow up thy soul; freeze thy young blood,
> Make thy two eyes like stars start from their spheres;
> And each particular hair to stand on end
> Like quills upon the fretful porcupine."

In writing the following description of Salisbury, I do not intend to describe the horrors of the place more than is absolutely necessary to set forth the scenes enacted. In writing this short account of my prison life in the South, I do not expect to produce much of a literary work, but merely a simple, truthful story of life in this southern prison. I claim but one merit for this narration and that is truth. I will be willing to answer for it on the day of final accounting. No tongue can express, no pen can describe the sufferings of the inmates of the prisons of the South. It is only through the experience given to the public by the survivors that this chilling part of the history of the Civil War has become known. No chapter in the Civil War is so imperfectly understood as the one relating to the military prisons of the South. Only the survivors of this hellish cataclysm can begin to tell this tale, but I fear that even our words will fail to accurately describe the agony, wretchedness and misery endured at Salisbury.

In Salisbury alone, over twelve thousand prisoners, who were in the prime of life, strong, robust and healthy, perished. And in all the southern prisons, as near as can be ascertained, about seventy thousand men fell victims to rebel brutality. To Jefferson Davis and his advisors, cabinet and the cruel men sent to run these prisons belongs the infamy of perpetrating one of the most horrible crimes known in the history of the world, and one that will forever remain a blot and stigma on that page of our country's history.

The prison at Salisbury was for some time a "palace" as compared to other pens, but 'ere long it degenerated into one of the worst. The prison yard covered some four acres, and was surrounded by a high board fence. A few tents were set up in the yard, but when the number of prisoners increased into the thousands there was not shelter enough for one-half of them. Thousands were exposed to the weather, day and night, throughout the entire winter, and in the majority of the cases the men possessed neither overcoat nor blanket, not even a blouse nor shoes. In a condition of seminudity we burrowed in the earth, crept under buildings or worried through the chilly December nights in the open air, lying unsheltered upon the muddy, frozen or snowy ground. To see men suffering in this manner was a sight piteous beyond description.

The rations were one pint of cornmeal, cob included, and one pint called rice or bean soup, once a day, without salt, perhaps even more scanty. The men were organized into divisions of one thousand each, and the divisions were subdivided into squads of one hundred. It was our daily occurrence that one or more divisions were kept without a mouthful of food for twenty-four hours, and in some cases as long as forty-eight hours. The prisoners sold every scrap of their personal belongings, often down to the shirts on their backs, to obtain money to buy bread, and it took from five to twenty dollars of Confederate money to buy one small loaf. At this very time the commissary warehouse in Salisbury was packed to the roof with corn and pork and this starvation of the prisoners was a deliberate and willful cruelty enforced by Major John H. Gee, the post commandant. When Gee was asked by a subordinate for permission to give more food to the prisoners this "chivalrous" product of Southern civilization replied, "No, damn them. Give them quarter rations!"

To call the filthy pens where the sick soldiers were confined "hospitals," is a perversion of the English language. A better term would be "slaughterhouses," which is what the Salisbury inmates themselves called them. Long, low structures averaging twenty-five by seventy feet, some of brick and others of logs, they were unattractive without and unspeakably horrible within. The sick and dying prisoners lay in rows of ghastly near skeletons. Wasted forms, sad and pleading eyes, sobs of sorrow and wails of despair, awful and constant hacking of coughs. There was blood and filth everywhere. The air was both stale and stifling. The dead wagon filled with loads of stiffening corpses piled in like cordwood, the arms and legs swaying with the motion of the cart, with pitiful white-eyed staring specters, rattled along to the trenches outside to hastily dump their human debris into a few inches of unhallowed dirt. There was pain everywhere. I recall seeing legions of sunken eyes and sullen despondency, the precursors of almost certain death.

On a raw December day with the ground half filled with slush and snow and freezing rain falling steadily more than six thousand prisoners were unable to find any shelter. I huddled shoeless, half-naked and hollow-eyed with my comrades around a fire of green and smoky wood in a crowded tent. Men wrapped their arms outside chimneys desperately trying to extract some warmth from the half-heated bricks. Others curled up in narrow caves while burning pine filled our eyes with smoke without warming our numb bodies. We stood with pallid cheeks and wistful eyes, begging for admission even into those "slaughter pens" where our sick comrades were lying in dirt, distress and despair. Night came bringing more misery from coldness. Men fell down wherever chance afforded, and huddled together for mutual warmth. I was one of a dozen wretches in a trench that night. At sunrise some of us managed to arise to resume our weary tramp, but many lay frozen stiff.

Before I conclude my account of the sufferings at the Salisbury prison camp I must discuss the November massacre in some detail. Without deliberation or concert, but acting solely upon a momentary impulse, a portion of the prisoners made a desperate, ill-advised and futile effort to escape from bondage. We had gone without food again for forty-eight hours and were weak and desperate. As a rebel relief column of sixteen men arrived at noon in the prison yard the strongest of the most desperate prisoners, armed with clubs, sprang upon them. The rebs were surprised and quickly disarmed. One guard resisted and was killed with a bayonet thrust. The other rushed away and gave the alarm. The prisoners rushed to one part of the enclosure hoping to climb the walls to freedom. In less than three minutes every musket in the garrison was turned upon us and two or three field pieces hurled grape and canister into the struggling throng. In minutes one hundred and fifteen men lay dead on the ground. Most were innocent bystanders struck dead in the melee. Many men died in lingering agony.

Death was everywhere at Salisbury. Black prisoners were the favorite targets of rebel guards. Many black soldiers were murdered on the pretext of having strayed too closely to the walls. White soldiers shared their fate on many an occasion.

Captain Wirz, second in command at Salisbury, had the practice of mounting the stockade and addressing the starving prisoners. "All you Yankee prisoners who want to take the oath to the Confederate States of America will please come up close to the small gate here, and go out into a good clean camp, and have plenty to eat!" Less than five percent of the men accepted this offer.

Men who had cheerfully faced death on many a battlefield, lay down and died brokenhearted, as the terrible suspicion forced itself into their minds that the government they loved so well and had fought so hard to save, was indifferent to their sad fate. Dying at a rate of more than fifty per day they remained loyal to the old flag. A great army of these, and many of them my near and dear friends, passed away to the great beyond. We left their frail bodies and they were buried in a strange land. They quietly sleep where the woodbine twineth. The weary are now at rest. I have but one tribute to offer, prayers for the living, tears for the dead.

On one occasion, a mere boy belonging to my company, Perry Hickman, whose home was in Newtown, Whiteley Township, Greene County, Pennsylvania, died. As gently and quietly as falls the autumn leaf, his pure spirit left his tortured body and winged its way to a better and more blissful land.

> "Matted and damp are the curls of gold
> Kissing the snow of the fair young brow.
> Pale are the lips of delicate mould,-
> Somebody's darling is dying now.
> Back from the beautiful blue veined brow,
> Brush all the wandering waves of gold;
> Cross his hands on his bosom now.
> Somebody's darling is still and cold."

At Salisbury, the following members of my company, all from Greene County died as if they were sleeping: Clark Burk, William Watson, William Funk, Marian Morris and David Keys. They were loyal to their country and died that the nation might live. May the principles of true fidelity be a living monument to their memory. In December, 1864, and January, 1865, the death rate at Salisbury was from fifty to seventy-five per day. Many a poor soul found relief from these torments by a swift bullet from the guards. My own life was in jeopardy on five occasions by them. I once enraged a Johnnie reb and he would have bayoneted me but for my comrades providing a protective circle about my person. Twice I was nearly killed by bullets and once by the butt of a rifle. On another occasion I was nearly killed by a stray bullet which narrowly missed my head.

After the Civil War Captain Wirz and Lieutenant Davis paid the penalty of their crimes on the scaffold, but John H. Gee, of Salisbury, went scot free.

On February 21, 1865, a rebel officer entered the stockade and ordered all the sick in the hospitals to be put in readiness for transport in the boxcars. All prisoners who were not able to march would get ready to be shipped with the sick from the hospitals by way of Richmond. At noon all of the sick were taken out of the stockade and tenderly placed in boxcars. After the sick came all the men who were just able to walk to the train. Soon the long train of boxcars left the Salisbury prison. Many of us left behind looked upon our fortunate comrades with jealousy. Others gave thanks to the Heavenly Father for their deliverance. As skeletons in rags left the gates of Salisbury you would perhaps hear, "Goodbye John, until we meet again. Tell my mother I am still living and hope to be home soon." Then the gates of the prison were closed upon the prisoners who remained to march out the next day.

That evening we were given three day's rations, consisting of one loaf of bread and one pound of pork. I ate my ration before morning came. Now housed in the old shelter tent we were placed in the previous November we numbered only fifty men. During this sleepless night, Sergeant M. Hazen called the roll. One of our fifty joined the rebels and thirty-eight more died. They quietly sleep.

At daylight on Washington's birthday, the drum beat for the assembly of the prisoners for perhaps the last time. We were ordered to fall into two ranks and take the parole, not to straggle or try to escape. We were to be paroled at Goldsboro. I left the prison with the aid of two canes having just emerged from a long spell of typhoid fever. We tramped towards Greensboro, North Carolina. I was frail and weak. When we stopped at night to rest in a barn my old friend James Eberhart procured me as comfortable a place as he could. During the night a prison thug attacked and nearly succeeded in murdering me, but comrade Eberhart saved my life. I will forever be indebted to him. I was suffering from scurvy and chronic diarrhoea.

On March 9, 1865, we arrived at Greensboro and on the 11th of that month filled a long train of boxcars. But suddenly the doors to the boxcars were all closed and the rain began to fall in torrents. A rebel Lieutenant approached me with sabre drawn in the darkness. Calling to me he said, "What are you here for and what are you doing here at this time?" I informed him I was so weak I could not get here any sooner, that I started with my comrades and my wish was to go with my messmates but I could not reach the train sooner. My words must have softened his heart. He told me to follow him. He stopped in front of a car door and pounding with his sabre called for it to be opened. The men at first refused, but afterwards relented and I was helped by the Lieutenant into the boxcar. During the tramp from Salisbury to Greensboro, and to the sea, I was always accompanied by comrades Hazen, Vaughn and Eberhart. During the night we arrived in Goldsboro. I nearly died on the march and remember Sergeant Hazen aiding me after I was knocked unconscious having fallen on a tree stump, saying, "Good, he still lives."

We signed the regular parole on March 12, 1865 and the next day were inside General Terry's lines near Wilmington, North Carolina. After remaining in the city one day we boarded a fine ocean steamer for Annapolis, Maryland. We arrived in Annapolis on the 16th and stepped down the gangplank to a throng of people looking desperately for their loved ones. We could only shake our heads. We were washed in the bathhouse at the capital city of "My Maryland," put clean clothes on and received two months extra pay and a thirty day furlough. On the 18th of March I arrived at my sister's home in Blacksville, West Virginia. After months of suffering with typhoid pneumonia, hovering between life and death, I have been permitted to drag along these years since with a broken constitution.

C. H. Golden

INDEX

A

African-American soldiers, 6, 27, 28, 174
Alabama, 17
Alexandria (VA), 21, 23, 24, 26, 30, 37, 59-61, 65, 67, 70, 105
Allegheny City (PA), 7
Allegheny River (PA), 16, 83
Allison (OH), 7
Amelia Court House (VA), 101, 102
Anderson, Colonel, 102, 105, 109
Andersonville Prison (GA), 168
Annapolis (MD), 151, 177
Antietam, Battle of, 37, 45, 46, 48, 49, 51, 55, 132, 135
Appomattox (VA), 76
Appomattox River (VA), 100, 166
Aquia Creek (VA), 38, 42
Arlington Heights (VA), 154
Army of the Potomac, 11, 12, 17, 22, 49, 58, 70, 76, 84, 85, 133-135, 155
Axton, James, 52-55

B

Baer, 64
Baltimore (MD), 16, 17
Barman, John, 145, 146
Bayard, 59
Beach, Jared, 26
Beaver Dam Creek (VA), 32
Belle Isle Prison (VA), 6, 89, 91, 95, 96, 126, 132, 152, 168, 171
Bethesda Church, Battle of, 73, 76
Biddle, Captain, 35
Bierer, Captain, 49
Bierer, John, 8, 48, 49
Bissett, A. J., 166, 170
Blacksville (WV), 177
Bloomington (IL), 40
Boissieux, Lieutenant, 126, 127
Braddock's Field (PA), 165
Bragg, General, 166
Brown, John, 168
Brownsville (PA), 54
"Buck Tails," 55, 82, 127
Bull Run, 1st Battle of, 16, 17
Bull Run, 2nd Battle of, 5, 6, 43
Bureau of Pensions, 8
Burk, Clark, 175
Burnside, General Ambrose, 23, 49, 58-61, 76
Butler, General Benjamin F., 121, 122

C

Camp Copeland, 165
Camp Pierpont, 7, 18, 22, 23, 38

Camp Wilkins, 15
Camp Wright, 16
Canon, Mr., 103
Carle, Colonel, 79, 82
Catlet Station (VA), 24, 25
Central Railroad (VA), 104
Chancellorsville, Battle of, 84
Charles City Crossroads,
   Battle of, 34, 35
Chesapeake Bay, 151
Chickahominy River (VA),
   11, 32, 33, 105, 113, 133,
   134
Clark, Reverend John B., 7
Connellsville (PA), 71
Connor, Captain, 19
Cold Harbor, Battle of, 76, 84
Crutchfield, Richmond, 29-31
Culpepper (VA), 28, 67, 68,
   70
Curtin, Governor, 17, 70

D

Dante, 119, 146
Darby, Sergeant George W.,
   1-159
Darby, Sarah Hutchinson, 7, 8
Darnell, Calvin, 93, 94, 122,
   123, 129, 130
Davis, Captain, 156
Davis, Jefferson, 90, 108,
   128, 172
Davis, Lieutenant, 175
Dawson, Captain H. C., 15
Declaration of Independence,
   14
Deep Bottom (VA), 45, 133

Dispatch Station (VA), 133
Doolittle, Major, 78
Doud, W. H., 43
Drainsville, Battle of, 76
Drumm, Samuel, 40
Dunbar (PA), 122
Dunkard Church (MD), 47
Duryea's Zouaves, 32
Duvall, Claude, 17

E

Eagle Gold Mines (VA), 26
Early, General Jubal, 112
Eberhart, Sergeant James, 54,
   152-154, 176, 177
Eighth Pennsylvania, 5, 8, 16,
   18, 160-162
Eighth Texas, 46
Eislie, Cyrus, 56, 57
Elsworth, 26
Emancipation Proclamation,
   143
England, 68
Erie Regiment, 15

F

Fairfax County (VA), 66
Fair Oaks, Battle of, 134
Falmouth (VA), 25
Farquier (locomotive), 24
Fayette County (PA), 5, 8
Fayette Guards, 15
Fell, Mr., 15
Fogle, Private, 129
Fort Harrison, 121, 129
Fort Pennsylvania, 17

Fortress Monroe, 38, 151
Fort Sumter, 13, 14, 36, 143
Fort Warren, 83
Fostoria (OH), 88
Fourth Pennsylvania Cavalry, 139
Francis, Leslie, 122-124
Franklin, General, 59
Fredericksburg, Battle of, 21
Fredericksburg (VA), 25, 27, 42, 44, 55, 56, 58-60, 65, 71, 76, 84, 106, 113, 116, 117
Fremont, General, 133
Funk, William, 175

G

Gaines' Mill, Battle of, 28, 32, 35, 45, 76, 133, 134
"Galena," 36
Gardner, Major T. B., 15
Gardner, Brigadier General, 105
Gaskell, Bud, 18-21, 37-39, 51, 60, 61, 63
Gee, Major John H., 173, 175
General Hospital No. 21 (VA), 130, 144, 147, 150
Georgia, 81
Golden, C. H., 8, 165-177
Graham, Paul, 139
Grant, General Ulysses S., 68, 70, 76, 97, 166
Greene County (PA), 167, 175
Greensboro (NC), 176, 177
Grindstone (PA), 122

H

Hanover Junction (VA), 104, 115, 118, 133, 134
"hardtack," 25
Hardy, Frank, 104-106, 108, 109, 117, 119
Harper's Ferry muskets, 16, 32, 107, 133
Harper's Ferry (WV), 84
Harrah, Joseph R., 165
Harrisburg (PA), 16, 154
Harrison's Landing (VA), 11, 35, 36, 38, 42
Hayes, Colonel George S., 18-20, 22, 23, 32, 35, 39
Hazen, Sergeant M., 176, 177
Heintzelman, General, 134
Hetherington, Captain, 105, 109
Hickman, Perry, 175
Hooker, General Joseph, 44, 49
Hornbeck, Hiram, 140

I

Insane Hospital (Washington DC), 18

J

Jackson, General Thomas "Stonewall," 43, 133, 135
James River (VA), 34-36, 77, 142, 168
Jetersville (VA), 101
Jones, Commodore, 17

Jones, Jeremiah B., 64, 65
Jones, Jerry, 28

K

Kane, Patrick, 148
Kearny, General Philip, 135
Kendall, William, 32
Keys, David, 175
King, 144
King, Doctor James, 5

L

Lee, General Robert E., 11, 42-44, 48, 50, 84, 101, 112, 121, 122, 133, 135, 165
Leithhead, Sergeant W. H., 43
Libby Prison (VA), 6, 88, 94, 95, 104, 107, 108, 119, 121-132, 140-142, 167, 168, 171
Ligonier Valley (PA), 139
Lincoln, President Abraham, 13, 132
Little Round Top (Gettysburg, PA), 70

M

MacQuilton, Second Lieutenant, H. H., 15
Magruder, 133, 134
Mahone, General, 87
Malone, General J., 123
Malone, J., 83

Malvern Hill, Battle of, 11, 35, 134
Manchester (VA), 89
Manassas (VA), 23, 24, 43
"Marengo," (steamboat), 15
Marietta (OH), 44
Marye's Heights (VA), 58
Maryland Campaign, 8, 49
Massachusetts, 78, 80, 82, 138
Massillon (OH), 144
McCall, General, 33-35, 133
McClellan, General George B., 8, 11, 29, 33-35, 48-50, 84, 111, 113, 132-134, 149
McClosky, John, 88
McDowell, General, 14
McLain, Colonel, 15
Meade, General George G., 42, 49, 59
Mechanicsville, Battle of, 29, 35, 76, 133, 134
Memphis (TN), 54
Millen Prison (GA), 168
Miller, M. P., 17, 18
Mississippi River, 54
Mitchell, Isaac N., 87, 98, 123, 129
Mitchell, William R., 64, 65
"Monitor," 36
"Monkey Turners," 55
Monongahela River (PA), 38
Moore, Sergeant Isaac A., 5, 93
Morrell's Division, 34
Morris, Marian, 175
Morse, Albert, 137-139

Mosby, Colonel, 26, 107, 116, 117, 129

N

"New Brunswick," 38
New England, 14
New Haven (PA), 122
Newmarket, Battle of, 34
Newtown (PA), 175
New York, 94, 140
"nigger peas," 95
Ninth Pennsylvania Reserves, 46
North Anna River (VA), 72
North Carolina, 110

O

O'Brian, 130
Oliphant, Lieutenant Colonel S. D., 15
One Hundred and Ninety-First Pennsylvania, 163-165

P

Pacific Ocean, 14
Pamunkey River (VA), 29
Parshall, Family of, 70
Patterson, Second Lieutenant H. H., 15
Peninsular Campaign, 28, 38, 42, 132
Perryopolis (PA), 122
persimmon beer, 67

Petersburg (VA), 28, 70, 77, 81, 83, 84, 87, 88, 123, 165, 166
Pittsburgh (PA), 7, 8, 12, 15, 16, 154, 165
Pope, Major General, 43
Porter, General Fitz-John, 43
Potomac River, 17, 18, 37, 48, 49, 55, 63
Proud, George, 32

R

Raleigh (NC), 152
Ramsey, First Lieutenant S. B., 15
Ramsey, General, 73, 75
Ramsey, Lieutenant Jesse B., 41, 69
Rappahannock River (VA), 26, 28, 60
Rappahannock Station (VA), 42
Rathburn, Doctor, 145
Reno, General, 44
Reynolds, General, 35, 55
"Richmond Dispatch," (VA), 122
Richmond (VA), 11, 50, 72, 89, 94, 96, 99, 102-104, 108, 112, 114, 118, 123, 132, 134, 138, 142, 147, 149, 150, 152, 167, 170, 176
Ritchie, David, 40, 44, 52, 64, 66, 71, 78, 88, 93, 94, 122, 123, 129, 136, 141

Robinson, Charles, 140
Rockville (MD), 49
Rodgers, Captain, 68
Ross, John, 88
Ruffin, Edmund, 14, 36

S

Salisbury Prison (NC), 6, 28 54, 65, 94, 98, 145, 146, 152, 153, 155-157, 168, 170-177
"salt hoss," 76
Savage Station (VA), 33, 35, 133
Sawyer, 144, 146, 148, 150-152
Seals, James M., 170
Searight, Captain W., 15
Seven Pines, Battle of, 76
Shakespeare, William, 43
Sharpsburg Bridge (MD), 49
Sheridan, General Philip, 35, 135
Sibley tents, 61
Sisler, John, 70, 71
South Anna River (VA), 106, 115
South Carolina, 77, 138
South Mountain, Battle of, 45
South Mountain (MD), 44, 49
"sow belly," 25
Spencer rifles, 71, 88
Spofford, 105
Springer, 86

Springfield rifles, 32, 63, 133
Stewart, Sergeant, 25
Stoneman, General, 81
Sturgis, Joseph W., 40, 44, 45, 154
Sturgis, Second Lieutenant J. W., 15
Sumner, 33, 49
Swihart, John, 144
Syke's Division, 32, 34

T

Taylor, Guy O., 8
Tennallytown (D.C.), 17, 18, 20, 22
Terry, General, 177
Tredegar Ironworks (VA), 89, 90, 168, 170
Turner, Ben, 55
Turner, Dick, 88, 89, 121, 123, 125, 126, 129
Turner, Major, 94

U

"Underwriter," 138
Uniontown (PA), 5, 7, 8, 15, 48, 70, 154

V

Valley Forge (PA), 152
Van Dorn, General, 54
Vaughn, 177
Virginia, 14, 26, 61, 65, 73, 135, 165

W

Walters, Charles, 132, 135, 136
Warman, Bartholemew, 81, 122, 129, 136
Warren, G. R., 165
Warrenton, 42
Washington D.C., 37, 44, 49, 70
Washington, Mary Ball, 26
Watson, William, 175
Weldon, Railroad (VA), 6, 86, 165, 168
Wells, J. M., 43
Wesley, John, 13
Wheaton, General, 59
White House, 29
White House Landing, 33, 133
White Oak Swamp (VA), 33, 35
Wilcox, Samuel, 78
Williams, 83
Wilmington (NC), 177
Wirz, Captain, 174, 175
Wisconsin, 124, 140
Woodward, Mr., 130, 132, 136, 142, 150

Y

Yellow Tavern (VA), 28, 86
Yorktown, Seige of, 11

www.ingramcontent.com/pod-product-compliance
Lightning Source LLC
Chambersburg PA
CBHW050635160426
43194CB00010B/1676

9780788413070